C Programming

Principles & Practice

Boris Allan

Paradigm

Paradigm Publishing
Avenue House
131 Holland Park Avenue
London W11 4UT

©Boris Allan, 1987

First published 1987

British Library Cataloguing in Publication Data

Allan, Boris
 C programming: principles & practice.
 1. C (Computer programing language)
 I. Title
 005.13'3   QA76.73.C15

ISBN 0-948825-15-4

Printed in Great Britain by Hollen Street Press, Slough

Preface

This text is aimed to assist those who can program in some other computer language to come to terms with C. This not a text on structured programming but rather it introduces programmers to C.

C is an applications language which makes extensive use of libraries of functions, and C programs are basically collections of independent functions linked together. In such a situation there can be no fixed rules.

Originally, **C Programming | Principles and practice** (C3P) was aimed at a purely student market, but since working at the European Development Group of Computervision (Penn Street, Amersham, UK) the text has been used for inhouse C training courses. Programmers at Computervision have also used C3P as a self-teaching text.

The original of C3P was produced on a PC computer, and the ASCII files were copied into the Computervision CDS 3000 Workstation. The text was then edited by the Computervision Tech Pubs 3000 desktop publishing system: this book is the camera ready copy produced by Computervision's Tech Pubs 3000 software.

I would like to thank all my colleagues at Computervision for their advice and assistance, especially Steve Jones, Pat Terry, Tony Seculer, and all those who were participants on my C courses.

Special thanks to Carol.

This book is dedicated to my sister, Moira.

Contents

Part One :: Overview of C

Part Three :: Strings and pointers

Contents

. . . .

Overview of C

C Programming | Principles & Practice is intended for those who have some experience of computers and programming.

In Part One there is an examination of the main features of the C programming language. The programs presented in this part can be executed on a computer, and this is intended as a section for doing as well as reading.

Chapter 1

Elements of C

This chapter outlines the three basic elements of the C language, and shows a simple C program in operation.

Part One as whole (chapters 1 through 4) does not cover all aspects to C, but gives an overview. The accounts in these chapters are not intended to be comprehensive, rather the aim is to give a feel for the nature of C: that is, how the language hangs together. A more comprehensive definition of the language is given in an appendix.

C is a compact language based on a few fundamental ideas:

- ☐ A C program is no more than a function which can contain other functions;

- ☐ There is distinction between the form of an action and the result of that action; and,

- ☐ Computer memory is organized in an explicitly sequential manner for use by the C programmer.

We will start by investigating these ideas, but first the conventions used for typefaces in C3P (C3P is short for *C Programming | Principles & Practice*).

● Typefaces used in C3P

Normal text	Most of this book will be in normal typeface, such as this description.
Program listing	This typeface is used for program listings, and for references to C language items within the main body of the text.
Problem text	All problem text will be set in this typeface.
Program output	Specimen program output will be shown in this manner.
User input	Information which has to be entered by the user is shown in this bold typeface.

● Functions in C

A C program is a set of functions, all of which have an action and all of which can produce a result. A function always returns a value, though the value returned may be designated as void (that is, no value is returned by the function because the function has only an action).

Functions which are combined to produce an operative C program need not all be in the same file. In normal programming environments most C programs are produced by linking together functions from many files.

One of the files must contain a function known as "main": in fact, a C program is a main function which calls other functions. When a C program is executed, the C system looks for a function with the name main, and execution always starts with the main function. If there is no main function, by definition, there is no program to execute.

Every function used in a C program has an action, and produces a numerical result (even if the result is void). For example, the C statement

```
printf("%d", 4);
```

refers to a function `printf`, which will print the number 4 on the console as a decimal integer, as a result of the format string `"%d"`. `printf` is a function with a specific form of action. The statement

```
printf("%d", aVar = 4);
```

will not only print out the number 4, but will also assign the value 4 to the variable named aVar. The action of the statement aVar = 4 is an assignment and the result of the assignment is the value 4.

The action of the `printf` function in the case of

```
printf("Who are you?");
```

is to print the question *Who are you?*, and the result of that action is to provide a value equal to the number of characters printed. It is possible to assign the value, which results from the action of the function, to a variable: thus

```
aVar = printf("Who are you?");
```

will print the question, and also assign a value to aVar (equal to the numbers of characters printed).

● The arrangement of memory

The C language organizes computer storage as a sequence of memory locations, known as bytes. A name (or identifier) of a variable or function refers to a specific number of consecutive bytes, where the number of bytes is determined by the declaration of the type of a C item. It is important to distinguish between:

☐ The *name* of an item.

   ◻ In the case of a variable, the name refers to the value of the variable, as stored in the appropriate locations.

   ◻ In the case of a function the name refers not only to the value returned by the function, but also to the sequence of actions produced by the function.

☐ The *address* of the first of the consecutive locations in which the value is stored.

☐ The *value* of a variable stored in a sequence of locations starting at a specified address.

☐ The *definition* of a function which determines the instructions stored in a sequence of locations starting at a specified address.

● Simple C programs

Try to keep these three main ideas before you, as we start by looking at the simplest C program ever, which is probably:

```
main()
  {}
```

a program which does nothing.

There are two parts to the simple program:

`main()`	This line declares a function called `main`. The C translator knows that `main` is a function because the name is followed by the parentheses `()`. From now on, when I refer to a function in the text, I will add `()` after the name: this, therefore, is the function `main()`.
`{}`	This line defines the action of the `main()` function, declared in the previous line. The definition is empty, thus `main()` has no action, and produces no result.

A more complex (less simple) program is

```
#include <stdio.h>

main()
  {
  printf("Who are you?\n");
  }
```

which prints

Who are you?

on the screen. The principal change we have made to the simplest program is to the definition of the main() function, which now contains a friendly enquiry. That is:

```
printf("Who are you?\n");
```

(The meaning of \n is given in the next chapter.)

The portion of program between { and } is commonly termed a block, and within any block the separate statements are terminated by a semicolon (even though there is only one statement for this block).

The change to the definition of main() is reflected in another change, that is, the new line

```
#include <stdio.h>
```

an instruction to the C translator to include information from a file known as stdio.h. The new information is needed to accommodate the function printf() used in the main() function definition. Within the file stdio.h, there is a declaration of printf() (more on declarations shortly). The declaration of printf() in the file stdio.h is of the form:

```
extern int printf();
```

which states that printf() is a function (returning an integer) whose scope is global, that is, external to all functions (unrestricted). The inclusion of information from other sources (not always other C program files) is how C operates. Only the most primitive operators are intrinsic to C, and to perform any real work information has to be added or linked.

Chapter 2

Action and result

We have noted that any object in C has an action, and produces a result.

To illustrate some of the consequences of this distinction, here is an example of a short program which prints the following information on screen:

> *Who are you?*
> *Has 13 charactors*

That is:

```
#include <stdio.h>

main()
   {
   int whoCount;
   whoCount
      = printf("Who are you?\n");
   printf("Has %d characters\n",
      whoCount);
   }
```

The latest attempt is beginning to look more of a proper program.

● A proper program

In the above program first we declare that there is an integer variable named whoCount, and then we assign the result of printing the enquiry to whoCount (whatever the end result of printf() happens to be).

An integer variable can store only values which are whole numbers (positive or negative). The action of printf() is to print text, the end result is to produce (or return) the number of characters printed — an integer quantity.

The format control, %d, in the second printf(), means that the C translator is to print a decimal integer at that position in the string. A string is a sequence of characters enclosed in double quotes (that is, within ""), and a string is always the first (or only) argument to the printf() function.

The second, and successive, arguments to printf() provide values to be printed according to the format controls specified in the string given as the first argument.

Note that, apart from the string given as first argument, the arguments to printf() (or the individual parts of statements) can be on different lines. C accepts such separation by what are known as whitespace characters, as long as the names of items (or strings) are not divided by such characters. In the string

```
    Who are you?
```

there is a space between the two words: in this case the space is significant. In the assignment

```
    whoCount
        = printf("Who are you?\n");
```

the spaces and change of line between the three items are not significant, and the effect of the assignment is the same as:

```
    whoCount=printf("Who are you?\n");
```

In C, whitespace characters such as spaces, tabs, and newlines are not needed to delimit the separate items. Note that the space in the name on the left hand side of the next assignment produces an illegal name:

```
who Count = printf("Who are you?\n");
```

because C thinks there are two identifiers: who and Count.

● Counting characters

There are two small problems with the latest program to greet humanity:

[1] The text Who are you? has 12 characters, not 13; and

[2] Not every C system will return the character count for printf(), even though this is the rare exception.

The second problem is a a product of the vagaries of older versions of C, and standards for C are beginning to prevail.

The first problem is not a problem when we examine the way in which C treats strings, and in C strings are nothing more than sequences of characters stored in bytes.

The symbol pair \n introduced into the printf() format string

```
Who are you?\n
```

is known as an escape sequence. When the symbol pair appears in a printf() statement this is an instruction to move the cursor to a new line. \n is an invisible character (a newline character), but still a character.

We have to count the \n character in

```
Who are you?\n
```

even though the newline character does not print as a visible item. The pair \n is treated as one character, not as two. As a result, therefore, there are 13 characters. Can we ignore the \n in the count?

● Decrement operators

Consider the following (expanded) program, which removes \n from
the count of characters:

```
#include <stdio.h>

main()
  {
  int whoCount;
  whoCount
     = printf("Who are you?\n");
  whoCount--;
  printf("Has %d characters\n",
     whoCount);
  }
```

The new program includes a very important new insight into the
workings of C, and in particular the distinction between action and
result. The important statement is

```
whoCount--;
```

which will be termed Version 1. The effect of this statement is
rather like the statement

```
whoCount = whoCount - 1;
```

(which will be known as Version 2). There are differences, however,
and the two versions are not directly equivalent.

The action of Version 2 is to take the value of whoCount,
subtract one unit, and store the answer in whoCount. The result is the
value after subtraction.

Version 1 of the assignment has a similar effect, that is, the
program prints:

Who are you?
Has 12 characters

The simple statement

    whoCount--;

is confusing to those familiar with most other languages, because an action and a result are incorporated in that one statement.

The use of the decrement operator (--) is common in C programming and in later chapters we will investigate the characteristics of both decrement and increment operators. If the above program is altered to

```
#include <stdio.h>

main()
    {
    int whoCount, newCount;
    whoCount = printf("Who are you?\n");
    whoCount--;
    newCount = whoCount;
    printf("Has %d or %d characters\n",
        whoCount, newCount);
    }
```

The printed outcome is

    Who are you?
    Has 12 or 12 characters

which is consistent, that is, whoCount gives the same result as newCount, if the value of whoCount is assigned to newCount. Suppose, however, the program is simplified slightly to take out an excess statement?

◉ Variations of action

The latest modification to the questioning program simplifies to the extent that one line has been eliminated. The lines

```
whoCount--;
newCount = whoCount;
```

have been removed, and the one line

```
newCount = whoCount--;
```

has been substituted. Here is the new version:

```
#include <stdio.h>

main()
  {
  int whoCount, newCount;
  whoCount = printf("Who are you?\n");
  newCount = whoCount--;
  printf("Has %d or %d characters\n",
    whoCount, newCount);
  }
```

The printed output is not as you might expect, because the text is

Who are you?
Has 12 or 13 characters

due to the distinction in C between action and result. The postfix use of the decrement operator (that is, -- follows the name of the variable) means that reducing the value by one unit occurs *after* the value has been used. The *action* of the postfix decrement is to reduce the value by one unit, the *result* is to produce the original value.

The order of operation for

```
newCount = whoCount--;
```

is as follows:

- ☐ newCount is undefined in value, and whoCount is equal to 13;
- ☐1 Assign the current value of whoCount to newCount (newCount is 13); and,
- ☐2 After the value has been assigned, decrement the value of whoCount by one unit (whoCount is 12).

This sequence can be shown schematically as follows:

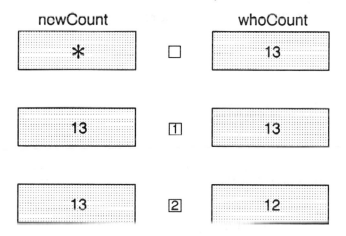

Thus the value 13 (the initial value of whoCount) is assigned to newCount, and the value of whoCount is reduced to 12 after making the assignment.

● A new decrement

If the key line is altered, a new program is produced, with a different result:

```
#include <stdio.h>

main()
    {
    int whoCount, newCount;
    whoCount = printf("Who are you?\n");
    newCount = --whoCount;
    printf("Has %d or %d characters\n",
        whoCount, newCount);
    }
```

producing the output text

> *Who are you?*
> *Has 12 or 12 characters*

The action of the prefix decrement operator is exactly the same as that for the postfix use, but the result is the decremented value. So, for

```
newCount = --whoCount;
```

the sequence is:

☐ newCount is undefined in value, and whoCount is equal to 13;

[1] Decrement the value of whoCount by one unit (whoCount is 12); and

[2] Assign the decremented value of whoCount to newCount (newCount is 12).

Thus the value 12 (the decremented value of whoCount) is assigned to newCount, and the value of whoCount is reduced to 12 before making the assignment.

This sequence can be shown schematically as follows:

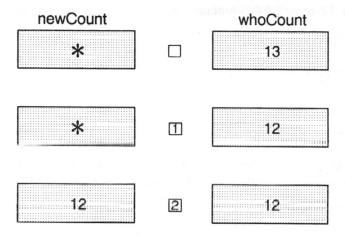

● Multiply and assign

Before we move to a discussion of data types, a final example: the combined multiplication and assignment operator, *= (one of a whole series of such operators).

```
#include <stdio.h>

main()
    {
    int whoCount, newCount;
    whoCount = printf("Who are you?\n");
    newCount = --whoCount;
    newCount *= 2;
    printf("Has %d or half %d characters\n",
    whoCount, newCount);
    }
```

This program produces the output text

Who are you?
Has 12 or half 24 characters

because the line

```
newCount *= 2;
```

is equivalent to

```
newCount = newCount * 2;
```

The action generated by *= is to multiply the value of the variable named on the left by the value on the right, and the result is the outcome of the multiplication (stored in the variable already named on the left hand side).

Chapter 3

Declarations and addresses

The data type for the variables whoCount and newCount, used in the previous chapter, is integer. That they are so designated is shown by the declaration:

```
int whoCount, newCount;
```

The int declaration sets aside a certain number of consecutive bytes in memory for each variable, and defines the expected type of operation for those variables.

The bytes set aside are used to store the value of each variable, where the number of bytes per variable is set by the declared data type. For many C systems 2 bytes are set aside for each integer variable or — in other words — the size of the type is 2, though for computers with 32 bit processors, the normal size of an integer tends to be 4 bytes.

The number of bytes set aside for integer variables will have an impact, of course, on the limits to the size of an integer for any particular implementation. The next program shows how C aids the programmer investigate the system in use, with the object of allowing that programmer to use the system to the greatest effect.

● The sizeof integers

Here is the program:

```
#include <stdio.h>

main()
    {
    int whoCount, newCount;
    printf("Size of whoCount is %d\n",
        sizeof(whoCount));
    printf("Size of newCount is %d\n",
        sizeof(newCount));
    printf("Size of printf() is %d\n",
        sizeof(printf()));
    }
```

The standard C function sizeof(NAME) returns the number of bytes set aside for the object with the specified NAME. In the above program, the sizes of whoCount, newCount, and printf() are examined, the printed output is:

Size of whoCount is 2
Size of newCount is 2
Size of printf() is 2

This output indicates that the content (in bytes) returned by all three is of the same size (printf() returns an integer value, as we have seen). Another use of sizeof() is

```
#include <stdio.h>

main()
    {
    printf("%d\n", sizeof("Who are you?"));
    }
```

which prints the value 13.

A character is normally stored in 1 byte, and thus the string "Who are you?" should extend for 12 bytes. The result is 13 bytes in the above program because the C translator signals the end of a string by adding an extra character, an escape sequence \0. The escape sequence \n represents a newline, and the pair \0 represents a null, that is, do nothing.

The C translator does not store the length of a string as such, so that the actual length has to be investigated each time a string is used. The length of a string is discovered by the translator starting at the first byte of the string locations, and counting through until the null byte is reached. The string starts at a certain (known) address, and ends at another (unknown) address.

● Finding addresses

An integer starts at a certain (known) address, as does a string, but the C translator always knows the number of bytes set aside for an integer. If two integers are declared consecutively (as are whoCount and newCount) then the addresses of the starting location for each integer will differ by two bytes (on many systems).

Here is a program to investigate the starting addresses of two int variables, firstInt and secondInt:

```
#include <stdio.h>

main()
   {
   int firstInt, secondInt;

   printf("firstInt address %u\n",
      &firstInt);
   printf("secondInt address %u\n",
      &secondInt);
   }
```

The & prefix to a variable name means we require the address of the first memory location at which the variable is stored. All systems are likely to differ in the exact values produced as output for this program but, generally, the values of the addresses will differ by two units or four units.

In the case of one C compiler on one system:

firstInt address 3572

secondInt address 3574

Note that in this program the `printf()` format control for the output
of values is %u. This format control means that the value is to be
printed as an unsigned (or positive) integer, because an address
cannot be negative in C.

The size of `firstInt` is 2 bytes, starting at the location whose
address is 3572, thus the next variable should start at 3572 + 2, that
is, 3574. We would predict that a third variable would start at location
3574 + 2 = 3576, because `secondInt` has a size of 2 bytes.

Nothing is ever that simple, so when we check by writing a new
program to investigate what happens when we mix data types in
declarations we find something new happens.

● Addresses and mixing types

In the following program we declare two types of variable (`int` and
`float`), with two examples of each type.

```
#include <stdio.h>

main()
   {
   int firstInt, secondInt;
   float firstFloat, secondFloat;

   printf("firstInt address %u\n",
      &firstInt);
   printf("secondInt address %u\n",
      &secondInt);
   printf("firstFloat address %u\n",
      &firstFloat);
   printf("secondFloat address %u\n",
      &secondFloat);
   }
```

We find that the text printed on the console is (for the system in use):

firstInt address 4068
secondInt address 4070
firstFloat address 4060
secondFloat address 4064

Thus it can be seen that for one system memory is allocated for floating point variables before that for integer variables (systems vary, so be wary).

Note that the starting address, for the locations at which values for variables are stored, is different for this program – due to the changed length of the program itself.

The new data type `float` has a size of 4 bytes. The `firstFloat` variable starts at location 4060, and has a size of 4 bytes, so the next variable (that is, `secondFloat`) starts at 4060 + 4 = 4064.

The variable stored after `secondFloat` is `firstInt`, which has an address 4064 + 4 = 4068, and `secondInt` starts at location 4068 + 2 = 4070.

● Arrays

Here is a program

```
#include <stdio.h>
#define PR(NAME) \
      printf("%u %f\n", &NAME, NAME)

main()
   {
   double aDbl, bDbl,
      cDbl, dDbl;

   PR(aDbl); PR(bDbl);
   PR(cDbl); PR(dDbl);
   }
```

which introduces a new data type double, and (far more interesting) a new C facility.

The double data type has a size of 8 bytes, and double stores fractional numbers to a higher degree of precision than float. The new facility is the definition of a macro, that is,

```
#define PR(NAME) \
        printf("%u %f\n", &NAME, NAME)
```

which defines a macro [1] to be known as PR, where PR takes one argument (NAME). A common convention is to give all macro names in UPPER CASE, and this is the convention to be followed herein.

A simpler macro definition (without an argument) is

```
#define WIDTH 80
```

which means that, whenever the name WIDTH appears in a program, the macro name is replaced by 80. Thus

```
printf("%d", WIDTH);
```

is converted to

```
printf("%d", 80);
```

by the C translator, using what is known as the *preprocessor*. The more complex macro PR(NAME) allows variable substitution for the argument.

That is,

```
PR(aDbl);
```

is converted to the statement

```
printf("%u %f\n", &aDbl, aDbl);
```

In the definition of the PR() macro, the solitary backslash \ at the end of the line is an indication that the definition is continued on the next line. The end of a macro definition is signalled by the end of a line, and thus — if the definition is too long — the \ at the end of a line cancels the end of line indication.

The printed output for this program is of the form

```
3982  0.000000
3974  0.000000
3966  0.000000
3958  0.000000
```

giving the addresses of the starting location for each of the four double variables, and the value of their content. Note that:

☐ the double variables have a size of 8 bytes;

☐ the memory is allocated in a reverse order of declaration (compare ints and floats above); and

☐ the variables are assigned the value 0 on declaration.

Do not forget systems will vary, so be wary.

We have four double variables, so why not declare an array of four such variables?

Here is such a program:

```
#include <stdio.h>
#define PR(NAME) \
        printf("%u %f\n", &NAME, NAME)

main()
    {
    double arrayDbl[4];

    PR(arrayDbl[0]);
    PR(arrayDbl[1]);
    PR(arrayDbl[2]);
    PR(arrayDbl[3]);
    }
```

for which the output is:

```
3958  0.000000
3966  0.000000
3974  0.000000
3982  0.000000
```

The addresses are exactly those of the previous program, but in this case the ordering is that given by the array index.

Note that

☐ The array index starts at 0 not at 1 — as happens with some other languages — and the reason for starting the index at 0 is not arbitrary.

☐ The declaration sets aside memory for 4 instances of arrayDbl, but the index varies from 0 to 3.

● Arrays and addresses

We can illustrate the importance of the index commencing at 0 by a new program:

```
#include <stdio.h>
#define PR(NAME,INDEX) \
     printf("%u %f\n",\
       NAME+INDEX, \
       NAME[INDEX])

main()
   {
   double arrayDbl[4];

   PR(arrayDbl,0);
   PR(arrayDbl,1);
   PR(arrayDbl,2);
   PR(arrayDbl,3);
   }
```

The macro is more complex in this case, and there are two arguments (NAME and INDEX). The expansion of the macro for

```
PR(arrayDbl,2);
```

say, is

```
printf("%u %f\n",
    arrayDbl + 2,
    arrayDbl[2])
```

and the printed output is

3958 0.000000
3966 0.000000
3974 0.000000
3982 0.000000

This is the same output as the previous program.

The implication is that the address of the first element of arrayDbl (&arrayDbl[0]) is given by arrayDbl + 0 (that is, arrayDbl). The name of an array (in C) provides a value, and the value is the *address* of the first location of that array.

The value of arrayDbl is 3958 (that is, the address of the start of the array), but the value of arrayDbl + 1 is not 3958 + 1 = 3959, rather (from the above program) we find that arrayDbl + 1 is equivalent to 3958 + 8 = 3966.

The calculation of the address of an element is

```
elementAddress = startAddress + elementSize * elementNumber
```

and for a double array the elementSize is 8 bytes. The C translator recognizes arrayDbl as a *pointer* to a location (an address), where the type of value to which arrayDbl points has a size of 8 bytes.

A *pointer* in C is a variable whose type is declared as being an address, and C recognizes the pointer type declaration as defining the action of arithmetic on the pointer variable. A pointer indicates a starting address, and the value stored at that address is returned by use of the indirection prefix operator * (known as indirection because the value is found indirectly from the address). Note that, for example, arrayDbl[3] is equivalent to *(arrayDbl + 3).

In the next program, the array is initialized on declaration but, because it is an array initialization, we have to use a form of permanent storage.

```
#include <stdio.h>
#define PR(NAME,INDEX) \
        printf("%u %f\n",\
            NAME+INDEX, \
            *(NAME+INDEX))

double arrayDbl[4] = {10,11,12,13};

main()
    {
    PR(arrayDbl,0);
    PR(arrayDbl,1);
    PR(arrayDbl,2);
    PR(arrayDbl,3);
    }
```

The C requirement for permanent storage is the reason why the declaration is outside the main() function. By placing the declaration at this position, the scope of arrayDbl is global. The declaration

```
double arrayDbl[] = {10, 11, 12, 13};
```

means that the array is of global scope, and that arrayDbl is initialized to the values 10, 11, 12, and 13. These values are integers and C automatically converts int type values to double type on assignment to the elements of the array. An alternative initialization would be

```
double arrayDbl[] = {10.0, 11.0, 12.0, 13.0};
```

which makes the initial values explicitly fractional and so no conversion is necessary to double.

   If a different file were to use the information about arrayDbl[], then that file would contain the declaration

```
extern double arrayDbl[];
```

which informs the C translator that the size of the array will be given somewhere else. Another way in which memory could be allocated on a permanent basis is the use of the storage class static (of which, more later).

The printed output from this program is

```
108  10.000000
116  11.000000
124  12.000000
132  13.000000
```

and the new addresses should be noted. The radical change in the start address is due to the changing situation of the declaration, to outside the main() function.

The expansion of, say,

```
PR(arrayDbl,3);
```

is

```
printf("%u %f\n", arrayDbl+3, *(arrayDbl+3))
```

where the meaning of

```
*(arrayDbl+3)
```

is: provide the value stored at the location to which (arrayDbl + 3) is pointing. The C translator knows that the value is of type double — because of the preceding declaration.

Note

[1]   A "macro" is a piece of program text (such as PR) which is replaced during compilation by appropriate program text. Macros will be examined in more detail in Part Two.

Chapter 4

Functions and arguments

Functions in C not only have an action, but also they have a result: if a function does not return a result, then the type of the function is void.

Arguments to C functions have their values copied, and that value may be changed within the function. As only a copy of the argument's value has been made, on leaving the function the argument still keeps its original value.

● Call by copy

This technique of copying values is known by many names, of which the most expressive is probably call by copy (or call by value).

The copying convention makes sense because the values of variables outside a function are not accidentally changed when the values are used as a function argument. The next program introduces several novel features.

In many programs we have to warn main() about printf(), and do so by the stdio.h include file. In this program we have also to warn the main() function about two new functions because main() calls two other functions, firstFn() and secondFn(), both of which are unknown to the C translator when main() is defined.

☐ As firstFn() returns an integer value (the default) there is no need to warn the C translator of the nature of firstFn().

☐ In the case of secondFn(), however, the function does not return any value (it is of type void).

We can refrain from declaring the type of secondFn(), because it is possible to assume the default without any problem, but for security it makes sense to declare the type.

```
#include <stdio.h>

main()
    {
    void secondFn();
    int xVar = 3, yVar = 1;

    printf("%d ", firstFn(xVar));
    printf("%d\n", xVar);

    secondFn(xVar, &yVar);
    printf("%d %d\n", yVar, xVar);
    }

firstFn(aArg)
int aArg;
    {
    return (aArg * aArg);
    }

void secondFn(aArg, bArg)
int aArg, *bArg;
    {
    *bArg = aArg * aArg;
    }
```

The firstFn() takes one argument (aArg) and returns the square of that value by use of

```
return (aArg * aArg);
```

thus an integer is returned. The default type for a function is int. The value of the variable or constant used as argument is not changed.

There are two arguments to secondFn(), and the second argument (bArg) is declared as being a pointer to an integer value (that is, an address). The square of the first argument (aArg) is assigned to the location to which bArg is pointing, by

```
*bArg = aArg * aArg;
```

The second argument is thus an address.

To modify the value of a variable, therefore, the address of the variable is passed to the relevant function. The address itself is a value, thus the *address* given as the argument cannot be altered, only the *content* of the locations starting at that address can be modified. Incidentally, the outcome of executing the program is

9 3

9 3

and it is worth trying to puzzle out why this is so.

● Controlling while ( )

We have seen how the situation of the declaration of arrayDbl (that is, in or out of main()) affects the storage of the values.

In this section we will look at one further form of storage (static), but the main interest is in the control of repetition: a program which searches through a list of values to discover the largest.

```
#include <stdio.h>
#define NEG(ARG) ARG < 0

int testList[6] = {5,4,1,8,13,2};

main()
    {
    int max(), index = 0;
    max(-1);

    while (index < 6)
        {
        printf("step %d max is %d\n",
                index,
                max(testList[index]));
        index++;
        }
    printf("\n%d\n", max(-1));
    }

int max(aVal)
int aVal;
    {
    static int maxVal;

    if (NEG(aVal))
        maxVal = 0;
    else
        maxVal = aVal > maxVal ? aVal : maxVal;
    return (maxVal);
    }
```

The storage class of maxVal is static in the function max().

Most variables declared within a function are local to that function (they have class auto), and this is the default. If variables are declared *within* a function (not as an argument parameter) then the default storage class is auto, that is, local to that function.

In most declarations within main() functions (in programs given above) the variables were local to main(), and it was only later that some variables were external to the function.

A local variable dies as soon as the function has finished, and if the function is called again a new example of the variable is created. A static variable in a function has a life which continues from one call of the function to another — its life is static. Consider this function

```
int max(aVal)
int aVal;
    {
    static int maxVal;

    if (NEG(aVal))
        maxVal = 0;
    else
        maxVal = aVal > maxVal ? aVal : maxVal;
    return (maxVal);
    }
```

The argument is aVal, and if aVal is less than zero [1], then maxVal is set to 0, otherwise (else) maxVal is set equal to the greater of aVal or maxVal by the conditional assignment (note the added parentheses):

```
maxVal = (aVal > maxVal) ? (aVal) : (maxVal);
```

If aVal is greater than maxVal then (?) return the value of aVal else (:) return the current value of maxVal. The value returned is assigned to maxVal.

If maxVal was local to max() (that is, auto) then, each time the function was called, maxVal would be initialized to zero (as with the declarations of arrayDbl[4] above). Making maxVal static means that its value is retained from call to call, so that it is possible to go through a list of values keeping track of the largest value so far.

It is possible to initialize maxVal by

```
static int maxVal = 0;
```

but by using a negative argument (it need not be −1) it is possible to reinitialize as required. Other forms of initialization and reinitialization are possible.

The function returns maxVal after each call, and if the argument is negative the value returned is zero (the function is reset). The declaration of max() as int is unnecessary, but has been given for illustrative purposes.

The max() function is used to find the maximum value of the values in the list of integers stored in the array testList[]. The successive values in the array are examined by use of a while–loop. In this case,

☐ if the index is less than 6:

   ☐ print both the index, and the size of the maximum element so far (found by use of max());

   ☐ increment the value of the index by one unit;

☐ check the value of the index, and repeat if necessary

The printed output is

```
step 0 max is 5
step 1 max is 5
step 2 max is 5
step 3 max is 8
step 4 max is 13
step 5 max is 13
0
```

and this should be compared with the list of values {5,4,1,8,13,2}.

⚫ Controlling for ( )

There are other ways to control repeated operation in C (otherwise known as iteration). For example,

```
main()
    {
    int max(), index;

    max(-1);

    for (index = 0;
            index < 6;
            index++)
        printf("step %d max is %d\n", index,
            max(testList[index]));
    printf("\n%d\n", max(-1));
    }
```

In this case, the for-loop encompasses everything we wanted from the while-loop, with a greater neatness. Note that the while-loop had two statements to execute, within the block

```
    {
    printf("step %d max is %d\n", index,
        max(testList[index]));
    index++;
    }
```

whereas the for-loop has only one statement, which was not placed in a block. Thus a block { STATEMENTS } (without a terminating ;) is equivalent to STATEMENT; (with a terminating ;).

● Controlling if ( ) else

Take the if–else control mechanism.

```
if (TEST)
    STATEMENT1 ;
else
    STATEMENT2 ;
```

where both STATEMENT1 and STATEMENT2 are single statements, each with a terminating semicolon — the else statement is optional. An alternative formulation is

```
if (TEST)
    {
    STATEMENTS1 ;
    }
else
    {
    STATEMENTS2 ;
    }
```

where STATEMENTS1 and STATEMENTS2 form a typical block. Note that the block (that is, from { to }) is not terminated by a semicolon (also the case with function definitions). The following text is illegal

```
if (TEST)
    {
    STATEMENTS1 ;
    } ; /* illegal use of ; */
else
    {
    STATEMENTS2 ;
    }
```

because the else is then separated from the if by an excess semicolon, and so the C translator thinks that the conditional is complete, that is, there is no else portion. When there is no else to accompany the if,

```
if (TEST)
    {
    STATEMENTS1 ;
    } ; /* no else */
```

is legal, though the final semicolon is unnecessary, because the semicolon at this point counts as a null statement.

● Controlling do while ( )

The other form of iterative loop is

```
main()
    {
    int max(), index = 0;

    max(-1);
    do
        {
        printf("step %d max is %d\n", index,
            max(testList[index]));
        index++;
        }
    while (index != 6);
    printf("\n%d\n", max(-1));
    }
```

That is, perform the operations (exactly the same as those of the while loop block) while the index does not equal 6. There is at least one iteration with a do-loop. At this point is worth noting that the statement

```
printf("step %d max is %d\n", index,
    max(testList[index++]));
```

is inadvisable. The value of the index is incremented within the
printf() function call, but the value which is printed as the first
argument (that is, the step) is not clear.

Depending upon the implementation, the value printed might be
the value of index before or after incrementation. The output for the
for–loop and the do–loop is the same as that for the while–loop.

⬤ Mathematical functions

Here is a program to work out the size of hypotenuse for a right
angled triangle, given the size of the other two sides.

There are two functions main() and euclid(), and important
features are numbered by use of comments (that is, /* */).

```
#include <stdio.h>
#include <math.h>                    /* 1 */

#define DIM(ARRAY) \
      sizeof(ARRAY)/ \
      sizeof(ARRAY[0])               /* 2 */

main()
    {
    float euclid(float, float);      /* 3 */
    static float                     /* 4 */
        x[3] = {1, 2, 3},
        y[3] = {3, 2, 1};
    int i;

    i = DIM(x);                      /* 5 */
    while (i-- > 0)
        printf("%f\n", euclid(x[i], y[i]));
    }
```

```
float euclid(a, b)
float a, b;
    {
    double dist, sqrt(double);        /* 6 */

    dist = a * a + b * b;
    return((float) sqrt(dist));       /* 7 */
    }
```

[1] Information is included (from the file math.h) about mathematical routines in general, and sqrt() in particular. The UNIX C command to compile the program is **cc prog.c -lm** . The information reveals to the C translator that sqrt() takes a double argument and returns a double result (see point 6).

[2] The number of elements in an array is determined by use of a macro definition which finds the total size of a data item (an ARRAY) and divides the total size of the ARRAY by the size of the first element of the ARRAY (that is, ARRAY[0]). By this means we achieve more generality.

[3] A user-defined function named euclid() is to be used, and euclid() returns a float result (and not the default int result). The more appropriate name pythag(), or similar, is already in use by some C math libraries, thus the use of euclid().

We have introduced a novel feature, because not only have we defined the type of the function but also we have declared the type of the arguments [2]. Note that not all C language systems will support the checking of function arguments.

[4] Two permanent (static) arrays x[] and y[] are initialized with 3 elements each. The reason why the arrays have to occupy permanent storage (with initialization) is due to the C translator's need to be able to allocate space.

In a later version of this program, we have to set the storage class of a structure variable (coordPairs) to static, because the structure variable is initialized.

5. The int variable i is made equal to the dimension of array x[] (that is, i is made equal to 3). The size of x[0] is the size of a float (that is, 4 bytes), and the size of x is the size of three floats (that is, 12 bytes).

6. The euclid() function uses an automatic double variable dist, and a library function sqrt(). The declaration sqrt(double) means that the function takes a double argument and returns a double result.

7. The double result returned by sqrt() is cast to a float value (by use of the (float) operator) before the value is returned from euclid().

The printed output for this program is

```
3.162278
2.828427
3.162278
```

and the program can be compared to that given next.

● Structures and pointers

In the program which follows we use a C structure. It should be noted that a C structure is not another variety of vector (or array). A structure is an assembly of items (or fields) which are collected together under a common name, and it is possible to have an array of structures.

```
struct Coords
    {
    float xField, yField;
    } ;
```

```
main()
    {
    float euclid(float, float);
    static struct Coords
        coordPair[3] = {1, 3, 2, 2, 3, 1};
    int i;

    i = DIM(coordPair);
    while (i-- > 0)
        printf("%f\n",
                euclid(coordPair[i].xField,
                coordPair[i].yField));
    }
```

The difference between this program and the previous program comes with the definition of a structure, called Coords (of two fields xField and yField).

The array coordPair[] is defined as being an array of Coords structures, and we write coordPair[2].xField to select field xField from coordPair[2]. The only real difference to the operation of the program is the association of the xField and yField values in one structure. For example, the call to euclid() in the first program is (in an expanded form)

```
euclid
    (
    x[i],
    y[i]
    )
```

and this can be compared to

```
euclid
    (
    coordPair[i].xField,
    coordPair[i].yField
    )
```

which is not particularly any neater.

In the next program we need only examine a change to main() and a (new) function hyp():

```
main()
    {
    float hyp(struct Coords *);
    static struct Coords
        coordPair[3] = {1, 3, 2, 2, 3, 1};
    int i;

    i = DIM(coordPair);
    while (i-- > 0)
        printf("%f\n", hyp(&(coordPair[i])));
                                                /* 1 */

    }


float hyp(coordPairPtr)
struct Coords *coordPairPtr;                    /* 2 */
    {
    float euclid(float, float), xC, yC;

    xC = coordPairPtr->xField;                  /* 3 */
    yC = coordPairPtr->yField;

    return(euclid(xC,yC));
    }
```

and the main points to notice are those commented by /* */.

[1] The address of the ith element of coordPair[] is passed as parameter to the new function hyp().

[2] The type of the parameter to hyp() is declared as a pointer (coordPairPtr) to a structure Coords. It is not possible to pass a structure as such as an argument, but it is possible to pass an address/pointer (and use ->, see [3]).

[3] The xField and yField fields of the structure are selected by the operator ->, so that, if coordPairPtr is a pointer to coordPairStruct, coordPairPtr->xField provides the same selection as coordPairStruct.xField. coordPairPtr->xField is equivalent to (*coordPairPtr).xField and is provided as a short form.

The call to hyp() within main() can be expanded to

```
hyp
    (
    &(coordPair[i])
    )
```

to clarify the action.

Finally, note that the structure coordPair[] could be initialized by

```
static struct Coords
    coordPair[] = {1, 3, 2, 2, 3, 1};
```

The dimension of an array of variables, an array of structures, or an array of characters (that is, a string) need not be given explicitly in a declaration. If this is the case, the dimension is signalled by some other characteristic such as an initialization. Above, we could have initialized arrayDbl[] by

```
double arrayDbl[] = {10, 11, 12, 13};
```

and the number of elements would be fixed at 4.

Notes

[1]   NEG(aVal) is expanded to aVal < 0.

[2]   The latest version of the ISO/ANSI/BSI standards for C encourage the checking of argument types in this manner, and thus it is the preferred convention in C3P. Unfortunately, many common C compilers (including most UNIX compilers) do not conform to this practice.

 If you are using a C compiler on a UNIX system then do not provide the argument types in this manner — leave the parentheses empty.

Part Two

Executing C programs

Any computer program has to be executed on a computer before we can derive any results. C is an applications language and, therefore, has to be able to use preexisting libraries of functions.

Only rarely is a C source program complete in itself — the simplest program uses `stdio.h`, if no other file.

This part examines the ways in which C programs are constructed, and how C language systems are designed to produce working programs from the original source language files.

Chapter 5

Starting C programming

The most effective way to learn C programming is by programming in C.

The most effective way to learn constructive programming is to engage in constructive programming in C, to solve significant problems. In this book (C3P) I concentrate on illustrating C programming by providing programs to investigate on your system. The example programs, and the exercises and puzzles, should be regarded as learning opportunities.

The emphasis is on you because, like most subjects, programming cannot be taught as such. Programming is something you can learn only by doing, like riding a bicycle, though the appropriate choice of examples can assist.

I try to use significant examples. What is classed as significant will depend on the stage reached, and I start with WELCOME. The program in this chapter is simple, but even simple programs have their informative aspects. With the simplest of programs we have to face in greater clarity many of the features of more complex programs.

By entering and successfully executing the example program you will have made inroads into understanding C.

Note that WELCOME is not the simplest of programs — the simplest program is that given earlier.

This chapter aims to introduce you to important aspects of C which may come as a shock to some programmers. In C, by and large, it is the programmer's responsibility to ensure that the program instructions make sense. It is this aspect of C which means that you have to know rather more about the computer than needed for most other languages.

In the case of some languages (for example, heavily typed languages such as Pascal, Modula 2, or Ada) the language translator checks to make sure that program instructions make sense according to specified rules. In C programming, it is up to you to know what you are doing, and why you are doing it ...

● The WELCOME program

The WELCOME 1 program is not too long to create many typing errors, but it is sufficiently complex to illustrate some major C features. There is a main() function and function starLine().

Try to enter this program on your system, to produce a correctly working program: in this way you will learn about your particular version of C. After the program has been executed successfully on your system, read on.

```
#include <stdio.h>

main()
    {
    void starLine();
    char nameString[80];

    printf("What is your first name? ");
    fflush(stdout);
    gets(nameString);

    starLine(40);
    printf("Hello %s\nWelcome to C Programming",
            nameString);
    printf("\n\nWelcome to C3P");
    starLine(40);
    }
```

```
void starLine(starCount)
int starCount;
   {
   int loopIndex;

   putchar('\n');
   for (loopIndex = 0;
    loopIndex < starCount; ++loopIndex)
          putchar('*');
   putchar('\n');
   }
```

This is the WELCOME 1 program, but there is no way that you can
know this is the name of the program.

In the above listing there is no information about the program
name, and the name is useful when you return to study past programs.
I need to comment on the program. The extent to which you use
comments when copying a program from C3P is a personal decision,
so omit all comments if you wish — though see the section **Comments
: an aside** in chapter 10.

● The production of a program

First, a few general observations about how a C program is created
and run.

Try to investigate the workings of your version of C on your
system, to discover how your system compares to the explanation given
below. Most C language systems have sufficient in common for you to
be able to execute all the C3P programs and examples with little or no
modification. The C3P programs have, in general, been written
originally for Microsoft C, but all the programs have been executed
using the standard UNIX C compiler.

The major differences in C systems occur in:

☐ the procedures used to convert the C program you enter, to
   instructions a computer can understand; and

☐ the library functions available to the user.

As C systems differ, first you need to establish how to create a C program, and the stages necessary to execute that program on your system.

All C systems have one thing in common: the original C program has to be created by use of a text editor or word processor (known generically as the editor). The program created by the editor is saved as a text file (the source code file).

Conventional C systems aim to take the source code program on file, translate the source code into machine instructions (stored in the object code file). The conversion from source code to object code is performed by the C translator [1].

After translation the object code file has then to be linked with other object code files to provide extra language information, such as the operation of predefined functions. The result of linking various object code files together is to produce an executable code file (that is, the program).

The total sequence from translation through linking to the executable program will be known as the compilation process.

On many C systems the complete compilation process is activated by one command — the system takes care of translation and linking without any user intervention. The one command facility is possible because most ordinary programs use only certain standard object code files (the standard library). Such programs do not need any special files (other than the program file itself).

● More about WELCOME

Here is the WELCOME 1 program, as given above, with the addition of an excessive level of commenting (some would say an "appropriate" level of commenting):

```
/* C3P WELCOME 1 program */

/* Boris Allan */

/*
 * Comments are shown in this manner. Note
 * that the program is exactly the same as
 * the earlier version, plus comments.
 */

/* Or like this */


/* Standard I/O library */
#include <stdio.h>

/* Main program function */
main()
    {

    void starLine(); /* Declarations */
    char nameString[80];

/* Input section */
    printf("What is your first name? ");

/* Clear the print buffer (stdout) */
    fflush(stdout);/* Input a character string */
    gets(nameString);
```

```
/* Output section */
    starLine(40);
    printf("Hello %s\nWelcome to C Programming",
            nameString);

    /* * */

    printf("\n\nWelcome to C3P");
    starLine(40);
    }
/* End of main program function */

void starLine(starCount) /* Function
                    with one argument */

/* Argument declaration */
int starCount;

    {
/* Declaration */
    int loopIndex;

/* Newline */
    putchar('\n');

/* Print starCount examples of * */
    for (loopIndex = 0;
            loopIndex < starCount; ++loopIndex)
        putchar('*');

/* Newline */
    putchar('\n');
    } /* End of function */
```

The WELCOME 1 program can be divided into three principal sections, indicated by the three following comments:

/* Standard I/O header file */

This is a directive to the C translator to include information from a special file `stdio.h`.

The file contains details about standard input and output functions, any necessary declarations, plus special definitions of the meaning of certain environmental features (such as the size of file buffers). The header file information is included in the source program so that, when reference is made to items such as standard input and output functions, the C system knows what is expected.

All C functions are implemented in libraries for specific topics and there are no built-in C functions as such. There can be a series of files (rather than just one file) included in a program at the start of the source code. All the included files use the `#include` directive.

Together with other directives commencing with a #, for example, `#define`, the analysis and combination of the information from the `#include` files forms the preprocessor stage (or pass) of the translator. At the preprocessor stage, the source program is treated as little more than a piece of text and — under the control of the directives — the text is altered to assist in later translation.

The C preprocessor facility is very powerful and of great flexibility.

/* Main program function */

When a C program is translated into object code, the system searches through the functions used in the program to find a function known as `main()`. If there is no `main()` function then most C systems will produce an error of the form

There is no main function

The purpose of the `main()` function will be examined in more detail later in this book. Within the WELCOME 1 `main()` function there are three main sections:

☐ declaring that a function `starline()` has a type `void`, and that a local variable name `String` is a character array;

☐ asking the user to input a first name, flushing the output buffer, and entering the name; and

☐ printing a welcome to the user, with the text being enclosed within two lines of stars (where a star is the ´*´ character).

/* Function with one argument */

The function starLine() is used in the main() function. There is
no value returned by the function, and so the function has type void.
starLine() has one argument known as starCount — an int
variable. Within the function there is a local variable, loopIndex (an
automatic variable). loopIndex is declared within the body of the
function, that is, the block between { and }.

    The action of the function is to move the cursor to a new line,
print a total of starCount examples of a star ('*') and, when all
the stars have been printed, move to a new line.

● Executing C programs

The result of executing the program WELCOME 1 will be to produce
text on the screen (the screen is the standard output device, stdout)
[2]. The first line to be output will be

    What is your first name?

because the function printf() will print the content of the string
enclosed in quotes. For certain systems the text will not appear until a
newline (carriage return) is printed, and so fflush() is a function
which clears (flushes) the output buffer. Flushing the buffer makes the
text appear on the screen.

    To the request for your first name, you should respond by typing in
a name at the keyboard (the standard input device, stdin). Let your
name be *Rhiannon*, so that the display looks like

    What is your first name? **Rhiannon**

where you have entered **Rhiannon**.

    The question and answer sequence corresponds to the portion
known as the /* Input section */ in WELCOME 1. If your printed
output differs from that given above, then the standard input/output
(I/O) facilities for your system are slightly at variance to the norm. In
other words, the standard I/O library (included at the time of linking)
differs for your particular C system.

    For example, after the request to enter your first name, the cursor
may move to a new line on screen, so that you have to enter your
name on a different line:

What is your first name?
Rhiannon

If this has happened it might be worthwhile to examine the
documentation for your system to discover the exact behaviour of
functions such as `printf()` or `gets()`. It is not likely that the
specified behaviour of either `printf()` or `gets()` will vary in any
major manner, but — with more complex library functions — there
may be slight differences in their action.

The next sequence of lines is sent to the standard output device
without any intervention on the part of the user. There are 40 stars, a
move to a new line, a greeting to you by name, and a welcome:

```
****************************************
```

Hello Rhiannon
Welcome to C Programming

which is the result of the `/* Output section */` up to `/* * */`.

The `printf()` function takes the string given as the first
argument,

```
"Hello %s\nWelcome to C Programming"
```

and sends that string as a series of characters to the standard output
device (usually the screen). The symbol pair `%s` is an instruction to
print out the string named as the·next argument (that is, that known
as nameString).

The component strings used as arguments to this instance of
`printf()` are

`"Hello`	Print out the text *Hello*
`%s`	Print a string whose name is given in the second argument (that is, nameString).
`\nWelcome to C Programming"`	Print a newline ($\backslash n$) and then the text *Welcome to C Programming*.
`nameString`	This is the second argument, the name of which designates a string.

A string is a sequence of characters explicitly enclosed in double
quotes (" "), or a string may be variable defined as pointing to the
start of a sequence of characters stored in memory.

For the command

```
printf("Hello %s\nWelcome to C Programming",
        nameString);
```

"Hello " is an explicit string, as is "\nWelcome to C
Programming", but in the latter case there is a symbol pair ´\n´.
The pair ´\n´ is termed an escape sequence, and this case is an
instruction to move to a new line. The variable known as
nameString points to a string, due to the earlier declaration

```
char nameString[80];
```

The declaration informs the C translator to set aside memory for
nameString, that is, storage for 80 consecutive characters (including
\0). The function gets() accepts an array of characters (a string)
entered via the standard input device. The string is stored as
consecutive characters terminated by a null character (that is,
terminated by the escape sequence \0).

Not all the 80 characters possible are used by the string
"Rhiannon", and the null character is used to establish the end of
the string. The string "Rhiannon" appears to be of eight characters,
but in fact is stored as the sequence

R h i a n n o n \0 ⁒ ⁒ ⁒ ⁒ ⁒ ⁒ ⁒ ⁒ ⁒ ⁒ ⁒ ⁒ ⁒ ⁒ ⁒ ⁒

where ⁒ indicates that the character is undetermined. The string has
nine characters (if we include \0) and the undetermined characters fill
up the remainder of the 80 locations reserved for characters — as
defined by the declaration of nameString.

The next printed output is that after /* * */

Welcome to C3P
****

The extra blank line is output because there are two newline
characters at the start of the string "\n\nWelcome to C3P" (that is,
\n\n).

Putting it all together I get:

What is your first name? **Rhiannon**

* *

Hello   Rhiannon
Welcome to C Programming

Welcome to C3P
* *

and if your display differs then your system may have varying definitions of the action of one or more of the standard library functions.

Once you have the WELCOME 1 program working successfully, try to solve:

PROBLEM 5.1

If a string is declared as

```
char exampleString[6]
```

then how long a string can be input by use of the function `gets()`? That is, what is the action of

```
gets(exampleString);
```

and what will happen, say, if the input string is 10 characters in length?

The solutions to most problems are given at the end of each chapter in a section entitled **Discussion of problems** and the problems are intended to be an integral part of the learning process.

First of all, try to solve the problem, to compare your solution with my effort(s): if you cannot solve the problem, study my account and then try to improve on the solution(s).

It is important to try to improve on the solution(s), because no person is able to get everything perfect at every (or any) occasion. Attempt the problem, the solution is in the next section.

▓ Discussion of problem

You will often find that the discussion of problems will introduce new aspects of C, but only because it makes sense for the problem being discussed. Note that I head this section **Discussion** of problem. I do not provide definitive answers, I merely discuss some possible solutions.

∷∷

PROBLEM 5.1

If a string is declared as

```
char exampleString[6]
```

then how long a string can be input by use of the function gets()? That is, what is the action of

```
gets(exampleString);
```

and what will happen, say, if the input string is 10 characters in length?

∷∷

As we have already seen, the string "Rhiannon" has 8 characters yet (when stored as the variable nameString) "Rhiannon" occupies 9 storage locations, because of the extra character (\0) needed to terminate the string.

   If exampleString is defined as being a maximum of 6 characters, then — as one character has to be \0 to terminate the string — only 5 characters can be stored as the variable known as exampleString.

   This supposition does not, however, have to be true. The best way to check the supposition is write a tiny program which uses the function puts() rather than printf(). puts(exampleString) is equivalent to

```
printf("%s\n",exampleString)
```

on many systems, though on other systems the equivalent function is

```
printf("%s",exampleString)
```

I assume the version with %s\n:

✳ IMPORTANT — DO NOT EXECUTE THIS PROGRAM

```
/* C3P PROBLEM 5.1.1 program */

/* Boris Allan */

/*
 * This program should be treated with
 * EXTREME CARE
 */

#include <stdio.h>

main()
    {
    char exampleString[6];

    gets(exampleString);
    puts(exampleString);
    }
```

This program should not be executed because possibly you will produce a system crash.

The reason why I have introduced such a dangerous program so early in C3P is that PROBLEM 5.1.1 illustrates an important feature of C. In general, it is the programmer's responsibility to check the sense of what has been programmed. Other languages are more concerned about checking sense than is C.

If PROBLEM 5.1.1 is executed, and the length of the entered exampleString is up to and including 5 characters (5 + 1 = 6), then all is well.

If, however, a sequence of (say) 10 characters is input, then it is likely that the result will be a surprise. It all depends on the C compiler, and the operating system on which the compiler is implemented. In most cases the string of 10 characters is printed on the screen (even though the restriction should be 5 characters), but in many cases the system then dies or produces a weird error message.

Now you have been warned, you may care to try the program for yourself, to see what happens on your system. On a multiuser system ask for permission.

Even on the same system, differences in the number of characters and differences in the characters themselves can affect what happens. If the PROBLEM 5.1.1 program is modified to provide a new piece of information it is possible to understand rather more of what is happening:

```
/* C3P PROBLEM 5.1.2 program */

/* Boris Allan */

/*
 * This program should be treated with
 * EXTREME CARE
 */

#include <stdio.h>

main()
    {
    char exampleString[6];

    puts(exampleString); /* new */
    gets(exampleString);
    puts(exampleString);
    }
```

If this program is executed, then the system behaves as before: the only difference in the running of the program is the result of the new line

```
puts(exampleString);  /* new */
```

which is an instruction to print out the content of the
exampleString.

Note that the new puts() instruction is prior to the gets()
instruction — thus the program prints the content of the string before
the string has been entered at the keyboard.

The first puts() will output a sequence of characters, usually
garbage. With some languages to declare a string also initializes the
string to some standard form (often the empty string) whereas, with
other languages, the string has to be given a value before it can be
used. With C, a declaration of a string is, in effect, a request to set
aside some storage for that string. The declaration

```
char exampleString[6];
```

is an instruction to the C compiler to set aside memory sufficient to
contain a consecutive sequence of 6 characters. The start of the
sequence is given by the value of the variable exampleString. The
declaration of a string has two purposes:

1 To set aside a specified number of memory locations; and,

2 To set a pointer to the start of those locations.

exampleString points to the start of the string, and the C system
does not know the length of the string.

A C function such as puts() finds the end of the string by
searching for the null character which is automatically appended to all
strings created. The puts() function starts at the location to which
exampleString is pointing, and then moves through the memory
locations until it reaches a memory location equivalent to \0.

The declaration of the string (an array of characters) does not fix
the maximum size of the string, just the maximum safe memory
available to store the string. One adverse consequence of this flexibility
is produced when there is an instruction to puts() and the string has
not been given a value.

The puts() function starts at the beginning of the memory
allocated to the string and continues until a null is encountered. As
the content of memory is indeterminate until the locations have been
assigned values, what is printed is garbage.

By entering a string which is longer than the declared string length, the `gets()` function deposits values in locations not reserved for the string. The locations may have importance for the system, and by altering the stored values it is possible that the system's behaviour is modified, often drastically. It is very important to remember that in C checks are few, and so care is necessary.

The lack of checks does mean, however, that experienced programmers have a very flexible language at their disposal. As you will discover, C encourages you to exercise control over the inner workings of the computer — little is hidden.

Notes

[1]   Another term is the C compiler, but the name compiler tends to have certain specific meanings for other systems. As C systems differ in the way in which the source programs are converted into object code, the name translator is more applicable.

[2]   In C, unless otherwise directed, input is considered to come from device 0. That is, the standard input device (stdin) number is 0, where the device is a generalization of the idea of a file (the device number is usually known as the *file handle*). Information from the input device is treated by C just as if it were from a text file.

In a similar manner, the standard output device (stdout) number is 1, and the output device is treated by C just as if it were output to a text file.

All error messages in C are sent to a separate device, and the standard error device (stderr) number is 2, though often the standard error output is directed to the same physical device as stdout.

On many C systems it is possible to redirect the input and output devices to disk files by use of the operating system. Redirection means that the same program can take input from, or send print to, a variety of devices and files without the program having to be modified. If the standard output device is redirected to a file then this does not redirect the standard error device to that same file.

Chapter 6

Refining C programs

In this chapter we will take WELCOME 1, and examine ways in which it can be improved.

The aim is to show how even simple programs can repay attention in terms of efficiency. Large C programs are normally little more than collections of small functions, and if each function has an efficient design then overall efficiency is improved. This, however, should not blind us to the importance of the overall design of the program.

Later in this chapter there is a short digression to introduce the use of logical operators.

A new WELCOME

Here is a small modification to the WELCOME 1 program:

```
/* C3P WELCOME 2 program */

/* Boris Allan */

/*
 * Use of call by copy in function
 */
```

```
#include <stdio.h>

/* constants (etc) defined */
#define LINEWIDTH 40
#define STRINGWIDTH 80
#define newLine putchar('\n')

main()
    {
    void starLine(int); /* Note argument */
    char nameString[STRINGWIDTH];

    printf("What is your first name? ");
    fflush(stdout);
    gets(nameString);

    starLine(LINEWIDTH);
    printf("Hello %s\nWelcome to C Programming",
          nameString);
    printf("\n\nWelcome to C3P");
        starLine(LINEWIDTH);
    }

/* Function with one argument but no auto. */

void starLine(starCount)
int starCount;
    {
    newLine;

/* Print starCount '*', using --starCount */
    for ( ; 0 < starCount ; --starCount)
       putchar('*');
    newLine;
    }
```

The main (and most important) difference between the two source programs comes in the content of the starLine() function, and even then there is only one real change.

There are two other changes:

☐ The use of #define is purely cosmetic in that the program structure is not altered, and

☐ the changed declaration

```
void starLine(int);
```

need not be used if your C does not allow the specification of argument types for functions.

The change to starLine() comes in the instructions which control the operation of the for–loop. The function (without comments) is

```
void starLine(starCount)
int starCount;
    {
    newLine;
    for ( ; 0 < starCount ; --starCount)
        putchar('*');
    newLine;
    }
```

Here is a direct comparison of the two loop structures (as used in WELCOME 1 and WELCOME 2):

WELCOME 1	WELCOME 2	
`for (loopIndex = 0;`	`for ( ;`	[1]
`loopIndex < starCount ;`	`0 < starCount ;`	[2]
`++loopIndex)`	`--starCount)`	[3]
`putchar('*');`	`putchar('*');`	**Body**

A for–loop is controlled by reference to three distinct entities, as labelled above.

● The structure of for ( )

① Initialization sequence

Commands can be executed in preparation for the activation of
the command(s) to be repeated in the body of the loop. The
two initializations given above are

□   (loopIndex = 0;
    which sets the local (auto) variable loopIndex to zero.

□   (;
    which does nothing, that is, there are no initializations.

If there is more than one initialization to be performed, the
appropriate commands are specified, with each command being
separated by a comma: for example,

   (firstVar = 0, secondVar = 1;

The end of the initialization sequence is signalled by the
semicolon, which separates this sequence from the next (test
condition) sequence.

② Test condition

Before each activation of the command(s) in the body of the
for–loop a test is made to find whether the loop action should
continue. If the condition is never true, that is, it is false at the
outset, the body of the loop is never activated. The two test
conditions are:

□   loopIndex < starCount ;
    The local variable loopIndex is compared with the value
    of starCount. If loopIndex is less than starCount then
    the body of the for–loop is executed. As the initial value of
    loopIndex is zero, the loop will always execute, unless the
    starCount is also zero (which is what is desired).

    It is clear that the value of either loopIndex or
    starCount has to be modified after each iteration of the
    for–loop — otherwise the loop will never end.

□   0 < starCount ;
    starCount is compared with the value zero and, if
    starCount is greater, then the body of the loop is
    executed.

The loop will always execute unless the starCount is zero:
it is clear that starCount has to be modified after each
iteration of the for–loop, so that starCount counts down
to zero.

There may be multiple tests, where each test is joined by a
logical connective to its neighbour: for example,

    (0 < starCount) && (starCount < 81)

which means that the body of the for loop is activated only if
the starCount is greater than zero, and if (in addition)
starCount is less than 81.

The && operator is the logical AND, with the other logical
operators being || (OR) and ! (NOT). The result is either 1
(if TRUE) or 0 (if FALSE).

3 Variable modification

After each complete execution of the body of the loop (that is,
after each iteration) values of certain variables may need
altering — especially those variables involved in the tests. The
two different modifications to values given above reveal one of
the most important aspects of C.

The two modifications are:

□   ++loopIndex)
    This command increments the value of the variable
    loopIndex by one unit. Each time through the loop the
    value is incremented and, when the value reaches that of
    starCount, the action is stopped.

At first sight, it might be tempting to consider the command
++loopIndex as equivalent to

```
loopIndex = loopIndex + 1
```

but, though correct in one respect, it is incorrect in another. For example, if the value of loopIndex is 10, then the assignment

```
newVal = ++loopIndex
```

will assign the value of 11 to newVal and the value of loopIndex will be 11. However, if the assignment is

```
newVal = loopIndex++
```

then the value of 10 will be assigned to newVal, whilst the value of loopIndex will be 11 as before.

The important difference comes with the positioning of the ++ operator. If in an assignment (say) the ++ operator precedes a variable's identifier, then the value of the variable is incremented before the assignment occurs. If the ++ operator follows a variable's identifier, then the value of the variable is incremented after the assignment occurs. (See **Problem 6.1** for some examples on use of the incrementation and decrementation operators.)

☐   --starCount)
This is a decrement command (the converse operation to ++). starCount is reduced from its original value to zero in steps of one unit after each iteration. When starCount is zero the for-loop stops.

If the function starLine() has been called with a variable (lineVal, say) as argument, rather than a numerical value, the value of lineVal is not affected by what happens within starLine(). All that starLine() can use is the copy of the value which is passed as an argument, starLine() does not know anything about the variable named lineVal. In C, arguments only pass copies of values, and do not pass names (known as 'call by copy' as compared to 'call by name').

The body of the for-loop is the same in both cases: putchar('*') , that is, send a * character to the standard output stream, without a newline.

::

PROBLEM 6.1

Here are a few examples of incrementation and decrementation
operators, to see just how well you can cope with their use, given
the meagre explanation above, and in Chapter 2. Assume that, at
the commencement of each line, the initial values of firstVar and
secondVar are 1.

What are the values of firstVar, secondVar, and thirdVar, at the end
of each line, if the relevant declaration is

```
int firstVar, secondVar, thirdVar;
```

It is only necessary to specify values for those variables which
appear in the line.

```
[1] thirdVar = firstVar++ - 1;
[2] thirdVar = --secondVar / firstVar--;
[3] thirdVar = secondVar / --firstVar;
[4] thirdVar = ++secondVar + firstVar--;
[5] thirdVar = secondVar-- / secondVar;
```

Here, completely without any preparation, is a line of code:

```
aVar = bVar * (bVar = aVar * 2);
```

If the value of aVar is 1, what are the values of aVar and bVar after
the command has been executed? Remember that it is probably
simpler than you think.

::

A slight digression about logical operators.

● Logical operators

The logical AND (&&), as noted above, is one of three operators: !
(NOT), && (AND), and || (OR). The ! operator has the highest
precedence of the three, followed by the && operator, and finally the
|| operator.

The relational operators (< <= > >=) have a lower priority than
NOT (!), but higher than the equality operators (== !=). The equality
operators have a higher precedence than the && (AND) and || (OR)
operators. Evaluation of a logical expression is from left to right for
binary operators of the same precedence.

Note that this precedence is the reverse of some other languages,
that is, AND often has a lower precedence than OR. Any positive value
is treated as true, but the value returned by a comparison (say) is
always 1 or 0 (TRUE or FALSE). Assume the following #define
substitutions:

```
#define TRUE 1
#define FALSE 0
#define EQUALS ==
#define AND &&
#define OR ||
```

The interpretation of

        TRUE OR FALSE AND TRUE

therefore, is not

        (TRUE OR FALSE) AND TRUE

resulting in TRUE, as with some languages, rather the interpretation is

        TRUE OR (FALSE AND TRUE)

also resulting in TRUE. The fact that the result is the same should not
be treated as indicating the unimportance of precedence. For example:

        TRUE OR FALSE AND TRUE EQUALS FALSE

which is interpreted as being TRUE. The association is

        TRUE OR (FALSE AND (TRUE EQUALS FALSE))

producing the sequence

        TRUE OR (FALSE AND (TRUE EQUALS FALSE))
        TRUE OR (FALSE AND FALSE)
        TRUE OR FALSE
        TRUE

The following sequence, which might appeal to some readers, is not correct

        (TRUE OR FALSE) AND (TRUE EQUALS FALSE)
        TRUE AND FALSE
        FALSE

As a check on what has happened, here are the two interpretations, as seen after preprocessing:

        1 || 0 && 1 == 0

This is interpreted as 1. The association is

        1 || (0 && (1 == 0))

producing the sequence

        1 || (0 && (1 == 0))
        1 || (0 && 0)
        1 || 0
        1

The other interpretation of the sequence is not correct

        (1 || 0) && (1 == 0)
        1 && 0
        0

Incidentally, the logical operators should not be confused with the bit operators & (bitwise AND), | (bitwise OR), ^ (bitwise eXclusive OR, XOR), and ~ (bitwise NOT).

To conclude this chapter, one more WELCOME modification.

● A third WELCOME

```
/* C3P WELCOME 3 program */

/* Boris Allan */

/*
 * Use of while-loop in function
 */

#include <stdio.h>
#define LINEWIDTH 40
#define STRINGWIDTH 80
#define newLine putchar('\n')
```

```
main()
    {
    void starLine(int);
    char nameString[STRINGWIDTH];

    printf("What is your first name? ");
    fflush(stdout);
    gets(nameString);
    starLine(LINEWIDTH);
    printf("Hello %s\nWelcome to C Programming",
            nameString);
    printf("\n\nWelcome to C3P");
    starLine(LINEWIDTH);
    }

void starLine(starCount)
int starCount;
    {
    newLine;
/*
 * Output starCount examples of '*'
 * Note the use of a while-loop with
 * a post-decremented argument to
 * test for the end of the loop.
 */
    while (0 < starCount--)
        putchar('*');
    newLine;
    }
```

The loop in the starLine() function uses an expression which incorporates a test and a decrement of starCount (though the decrement takes place after the test). This is a neat way of controlling a loop, and much the best of the ways we have been considering. The bare function is

```
void starLine(starCount)
int starCount;
    {
    newLine;
    while (0 < starCount--)
        putchar('*');
    newLine;
    }
```

It has been said by many programmers that the while–loop and
do–loop constructs are those which best suit C (which is not to decry
the utility of for–loop). After programming in C for a time, often you
begin to think in terms of while and do rather than for.

■ Discussion of problem

Here is a chance to be confused.

PROBLEM 6.1

Here are a few examples of incrementation and decrementation
operators, to see just how well you can cope with their use, given
the meagre explanation above, and in Chapter 2. Assume that, at
the commencement of each line, the initial values of firstVar and
secondVar are 1.

What are the values of firstVar, secondVar, and thirdVar, at the end
of each line, if the relevant declaration is

```
int firstVar, secondVar, thirdVar;
```

It is only necessary to specify values for those variables which
appear in the line.

```
1  thirdVar = firstVar++ - 1;
2  thirdVar = --secondVar / firstVar--;
3  thirdVar = secondVar / --firstVar;
4  thirdVar = ++secondVar + firstVar--;
5  thirdVar = secondVar-- / secondVar;
```

Here, completely without any preparation, is a line of code:

```
aVar = bVar * (bVar = aVar * 2);
```

If the value of aVar is 1, what are the values of aVar and bVar after the command has been executed? Remember that it is probably simpler than you think.

∷∷

We will take the increment/decrement examples in order:

```
1  thirdVar = firstVar++ - 1;
```

> The value of firstVar before the command is executed is 1. firstVar++ provides the value 1 to be used in the assignment, and then increments the value of firstVar to 2. The value 1 provided by firstVar prior to incrementation is reduced by 1 (that is, − 1), and thus the value of thirdVar becomes 0

> The outcome of the actions in the line is
> ```
> firstVar = 2
> secondVar = 1
> thirdVar = 0
> ```

```
2  thirdVar = --secondVar / firstVar--;
```

> The value of firstVar before the command is executed is 1. firstVar-- initially provides the value 1 to be used in the assignment, and then decrements the value of firstVar to 0. The value of secondVar starts as 1, then it is decremented to 0, the value used in the assignment.

The value assigned to thirdVar is 0/1 (which is 0).

Thus the new values are

```
firstVar = 0
secondVar = 0
thirdVar = 0
```

③ thirdVar = secondVar / --firstVar;

The original value of firstVar is 1, and --firstVar decrements the value of firstVar to 0, a value which is then used in the assignment. The value of secondVar starts and ends as 1. The value assigned to thirdVar is 1/0 (which is not a valid number) and thus a 'Divide error' should be produced, and the program terminated.

After the assignment, therefore, the values are

```
firstVar = 0
secondVar = 1
thirdVar = Not a number
```

④ thirdVar = ++secondVar + firstVar--;

The original value of firstVar is 1. firstVar-- provides the value 1 to be used in the assignment, and then decrements firstVar to 0. The value of secondVar starts as 1, then it is incremented to 2, which is the value used in the assignment. The value assigned to thirdVar is 2 + 1 (which is 3).

Thus the new values are

```
firstVar = 0
secondVar = 2
thirdVar = 3
```

⑤ thirdVar = secondVar-- / secondVar;

The result of this line depends upon the way in which your C compiler designer has interpreted the meaning of the operators. Either

[1] The decrementation of secondVar does not take place until after the assignment, in which case the values are

```
firstVar = 1
secondVar = 0
thirdVar = 1
```

(as the division is 1/1); or

[2] The decrementation of secondVar takes place as soon as the first instance of secondVar is encountered (that is, the leftmost secondVar), in which case the values are

```
firstVar = 1
secondVar = 0
thirdVar = Not a number
```
because there is a division 1/0.

This last problem is an example of how not to program: the expression secondVar--/secondVar is silly because it depends very much on how the compiler is written.

This is a case where side effects have been used. The use of side effects can be even more of a problem with complex examples: the moral is "Do not rely on tricks", because the tricks might work only on your system. Systems vary, so be wary.

The question about aVar and bVar was intended to take you unawares, and here is a short program to test what happens:

```
/* C3P PROBLEM 6.1.1 program */

/* Boris Allan */

/*
 * Multiple assignments
 * and what happens
 */

#include <stdio.h>

main()
    {
    int aVar, bVar;
    aVar = 1;
    aVar = bVar * (bVar = aVar * 2);
    printf("%d    %d", aVar,bVar);
    }
```

but — before running the program — try to work out what should happen.

Remember that, as with the increment operators, C distinguishes between the action of assignment and the result of an assignment.

For example, both ++zVar and zVar++ have the same ultimate action (the incrementation of the value of zVar by one unit), but the results differ in that the value provided by zVar is either before or after incrementation.

Parsing the program line

    aVar = bVar * (bVar = aVar * 2);

given above, to give a reverse Polish form, we find the sequence is

    aVar bVar bVar aVar 2 * = * =

As the translator moves along the reverse Polish sequence, stacking the values until an operator is reached, the order of execution is

```
aVar  2  *
bVar  (aVar 2 *) =
bVar  (bVar (aVar 2 *) =) *
aVar  (bVar (bVar (aVar 2 *) =) *) =
```

There are two assignments in the program line, and the first assignment to be activated is

```
(bVar = aVar * 2)
```

because it is on the right hand side, within parentheses. This assignment gives the value 2 to the variable bVar (that is, 1 * 2), but we are left with the problem that bVar is then multiplied by the assignment: that is,

```
bVar * (bVar = aVar * 2)
```

What value is used within the parentheses? All actions in C have a result, though sometimes the result might be a void.

Thus, the assignment to bVar produces a value equal to bVar (that is, 2). The second assignment is equivalent to

```
aVar = bVar * bVar
```

and so the new value of aVar is 2 * 2, which is 4. Running the program gives just that answer.

Chapter 7

The compilation process

We have not yet considered the ways in which a program is converted from the lines of instructions which form the program (the source code), to machine instructions which are executed by the computer (the executable code program).

Normally, we write a source code program and store that listing as a disk file (say, prog.c). The program we execute is stored as a different file (say, prog.o or prog.exe) and is the executable program file.

The question is: how do we get from the source code program we have written to the executable code program we run?

● The four components of a program

Rather than starting with the source code program, we will commence with the components needed for the formation of the executable code program. The four main components of the executable code program are:

☐ The original source code program.

☐ The relevant C language operations, as provided by the C translator, to convert the source code program to object code.

☐ The relevant standard (object code) libraries.

☐ The relevant user–constructed (object code) files.

That is, obviously, we must have a source code program. The program will be composed of declarations, definitions, preprocessor information such as #include, and must contain a definition of the main() function.

Figure 7.1   The   four components of a program

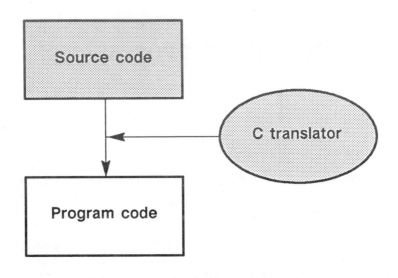

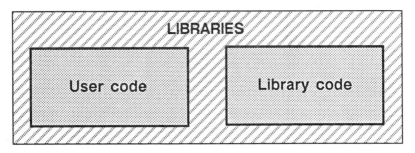

The source code program is written in C, and we translate the C instructions into machine instructions to produce the object code program.

Once we have the program code, the system needs additional information about some of the C language features used in the source program, because the basic features which are available as part of the C language are few in number. Most C programs consist of functions which are not intrinsic to the C translator.

Functions — not being part of the C language as such — have to be defined somewhere. Some functions are defined in the source code program; some functions are defined in standard libraries — the library code; and some functions are defined in user files — the user code. Both types of file are in object code, and are shown above as **LIBRARIES**.

This variety in the sources of information means that there must be a mechanism by which an executable program can incorporate (or link) information about functions from these object code files.

User files may possibly be designated as special user libraries. User files contain standard routines (and so forth) intended to be used by a wide variety of programs (for example, there may be a special library for bitmap graphics). Other user files may be written with the sole explicit intention of being linked with a particular source program to produce the final executable code file.

Library files (standard or user) should not be confused with header files, which are those files (usually with the extension .h) added to the source code file by use of #include.

● The linker

It is clear that an executable program is an assembly of disparate elements. The program is produced by linking together three distinct types of object code program (performed by what is usually termed a linker). It is important to emphasize that all three elements in Figure 7.2 are object code files.

The object code file corresponding to the original source program will be designated the program code. The object code file(s) which are standard libraries will be designated the library code. The object code file(s) which are converted source code (previously compiled by the user) will be designated the user code: user code files do not contain a definition of main(). The linker combines program code, library code, and user code.

Note that in Figure 7.2 the library code files and the user code files are shown within the box marked **LIBRARIES**. As far as the linker is concerned, there is no distinction between these two types of code file (even though, normally, the files are stored in different directories).

Figure 7.2   Linking object code to produce a program

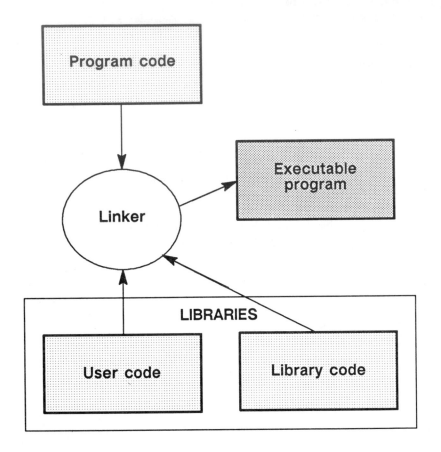

The principal difference between the program code and the user code is that the program code contains a definition of the main() function, whereas the user code files do not have a definition of main().

If there are two definitions of main() (for example, one definition in the program code and one in a user code file) then there will be an error. If a user code file contains a definition of main() then it is not really user code, it is program code.

As it is not possible to link two program code files, then two definitions of main() will produce confusion in the linker to produce an error and abort, but not all linkers respond in the same way to such a confusion. To repeat, a user code file is exactly like a program code file, except that a program code file has a definition of main().

::

PROBLEM 7.1

What happens if

1. There is no definition of main() in the program source code?

2. There are two definitions of main(), one in the program source code, and one in a user code file?

::

It is for reasons such as this that the design of a C program needs care and attention, far more care than needed for (say) Pascal. C is a production language for creating applications, and has to exist in the real world — Pascal was invented to help in teaching programming, and is a poor language in which to write applications.

By forcing you to structure your programs as sets of interrelated functions, C emphasises the importance of modular programming. It is perfectly feasible for a function, say, itemize() to be defined in a user code file and the function to be called in the source code.

Suppose you know that in a specific user library file there is a formatting function itemize(), and you know how the function operates. You wish to use itemize() to save writing your own version of the function.

Let there be an error during linking, where the error has arisen because (unwittingly) you have called a library function which does not exist. The name of the function (as defined and declared in the library) is itemise() and not itemize(). An error is flagged, but what happens when the program is executed?

●●●

PROBLEM 7.2

What happens if a function is used within the program source, but
the function is not defined within any of the (standard or user)
library files?

●●●

● The preprocessor

Having started with the executable code program and examined how
the executable code is produced by the linking of object code files, we
now need to discover how the program code is produced from the
source code program.

The generation of program code (or user code if there is no
main() function in the source code) depends on three main aspects:

☐ The use of preprocessor commands (such as #define),
declarations of variables, and definitions of functions, all of
which occur within the source code.

☐ Standard #include files such as stdio.h.

☐ User constructed #include files.

Normally, standard #include files contain only declarations of
variables, and preprocessor commands, but it is common for user
#include files to contain also function declarations. A #include file
is a text (or source) file which is included in (or inserted into) the
program source at exactly the point at which the #include directive
is issued.

In the WELCOME 1 program there was only one file to be included,
and that was the stdio.h header file.

```
/* C3P WELCOME 1 program */

    .


    .

/* Standard I/O function library */
#include <stdio.h>
```

```
main() /* Main program function */
    {
/* Declarations */
    void starLine();
    char nameString[80];
        .
        .
        .
```

and so on.

The name of the header file to be included is stdio.h, and the angle brackets < > indicate that only certain specific standard places are to be searched for this file (specified disk directories). If the header file name is enclosed in quotes, that is,

```
#include "stdio.h"
```

then the search for the file would commence with the directory in which the file issuing the #include directive is stored — if the header file is not in that directory then the search continues as with <stdio.h>.

#include is a preprocessor directive, and the stdio.h header file contains a fair number of preprocessor directives on its own account.

Here is an example of some of the preprocessor directives taken from a specimen stdio.h header file (stored in a directory known as INCLUDE):

```
#define   BUFSIZ   512
#define   _NFILE   20
#define   FILE     struct _iobuf
#define   EOF      (-1)
```

As we have seen, these are definitions of substitutions: whenever the C translator comes across the symbol BUFSIZ (buffer size), the value 512 will be substituted.

With nearly all C translators the translator goes through the program many times (it makes many passes), and after each pass the source is modified in some way to make the job of the next pass easier. The first pass is normally the preprocessor pass.

Further along the same stdio.h file there is a definition

```
extern FILE {
    char *_ptr;
    int   _cnt;
    char *_base;
    char  _flag;
    char  _file;
    } _iob[_NFILE];
```

which declares an array _iob of _NFILE elements, where each
element has the structure type FILE.

The declaration is termed extern to emphasize that the memory
allocated is fixed. There are similar declarations in other files, and the
extern designation is to stop confusion at linking (as there was the
confusion with the two definitions of main()). The stdio.h file has
to appear in all user code files, and so there will be multiple
declarations of, say, _iob[].

After the preprocessor pass (that is, after substitution), the
declaration of _iob[] looks rather different — in fact it looks like:

```
extern struct _iobuf {
    char *_ptr;
    int   _cnt;
    char *_base;
    char  _flag;
    char  _file;
    } _iob[20];
```

It is possible to see that where there was FILE there is now
struct _iobuf, and where there was _NFILE there is now 20.

Remember the #define directives? Remember

```
#define _NFILE   20
#define FILE struct _iobuf
```

for example? Notice that FILE was defined as being equivalent to
struct _iobuf, that _NFILE was defined as being equivalent to 20.

The preprocessor (on the first pass through the source text)
changed the text as directed. On the preprocessor pass, the translator
does not even care if the text is written in C or not. The preprocessor
looks at the text purely as text and obeys the directives, starting with
#, to process that text.

For example, here is a text file containing important information

```
/* C3P PreProcessor Example */

/* Boris Allan */

#define C3P C Programming | Principles & Practice

C3P is a book
by Boris Allan
about learning the C programming language.

So remember BUY, BUY, BUY

C3P

by Boris.
```

and after the preprocessor pass all occurrences of the pattern C3P are
replaced by C Programming | Principles & Practice. The
outcome of the preprocessor pass is the new text

```
C Programming | Principles & Practice is a book
by Boris Allan
about learning the C programming language.

So remember BUY, BUY, BUY

C Programming | Principles & Practice

by Boris.
```

with a good number of blank lines before the first line of text.
    These blank lines correspond not only to the blank lines in the
source text, but also to the comments and directives which do not
appear in the final text.

● Object code production

After the preprocessor pass, different C systems use a varied number of passes to produce the program object code. The fewer the number of passes, the more each pass has to accomplish. In essence, the stages of compilation from source code to object code are

   1 Preprocessing.

   2 Syntax analysis/language parsing.

   3 Production of assembler source.

   4 Conversion of assembler source to object code.

Preprocessing is always a separate pass, and is a fairly simple pass to understand.

After the preprocessor pass, the form of operation can become more complex. The sophistication of preprocessors can vary tremendously. For example, some preprocessors will allow #include files which #include files which #include files ..., others will not allow such nesting.

For some C systems stages 1, 2, and 3 are the responsibility of the C language compiler, and no more. In such cases an assembler source code program is produced, where the assembler listing is equivalent to the C source listing. The assembler listing produced (in a special file) is input to a separate program (an assembler) to convert from assembly language to object code (stage 4).

If you are using such a C system you may not be aware that that the assembler is being loaded, because the assembler may be activated automatically when you initiate the C translator. Here is a minor task: find out how your C translator produces object code program files.

••

PROBLEM 7.3

What happens if a variable is used within the program source, but the variable is not declared within that source code?

••

Note that if a variable is not declared there is a syntax error and thus program code is not produced — there is nothing to link.

The variation in action for missing functions and for missing variables shows the important difference between functions and variables.

On the one hand, variables have to be explicitly declared before they can be used in a program: functions, on the other, are considered to be defined merely by being used within a program. If a function is of a nonstandard form then it is necessary to provide an extra type declaration for the function.

For example, normally a function returns a value, and the default value type is an integer. The function gets() is a function which returns a value, but the value is that of the input string. In stdio.h, therefore, there has to be a declaration (external to the source file) so that the translator realizes that a different type is to be returned: that is,

```
extern char *gets(), *fgets();
```

Do not worry greatly about the meaning of the declaration at this stage, other than to note that the two functions (get a string, and get a string from a specified file) do not produce an integer as a result of their operation. The extern declaration is to stop the translator becoming confused.

As one further example of the action of the preprocessor, here is a line of code from the starLine() function in the WELCOME 1 program:

```
/* Newline */
    putchar('\n');
```

Within the stdio.h header file there are certain macro definitions used to amplify the meaning of putchar(). In fact, though it looks like a function, putchar() is a macro

```
#define   stdout   (&_iob[1])

#define   putc(c,f)   (--(f)->_cnt >= 0 \
            ? 0xff & (*(f)->_ptr++ = (c)) \
            : _flsbuf((c),(f)))

#define   putchar(c)   putc((c),stdout)
```

During the translation process, when the preprocessor encounters the

```
putchar('\n')
```

code, the line is changed to

```
putc(('\n'), stdout);
```

which is further converted (because of the macro definitions of both putc(c,f) and stdout) to

```
putc(('\n'),(&_iob[1]));
```

and the final preprocessed code:

```
(--((&_iob[1]))->_cnt >= 0
    ? 0xff & (*((&_iob[1]))->_ptr++ = (('\n')))
    :_flsbuf((('\n')),((&_iob[1]))));
```

At this stage it is not worth explaining the meaning of the expanded version of sending a newline to the standard output stream, but it is worth following through the exercise of macro substitution. Note that, as with the C preprocessor, you do not need to know anything about C to make the relevant substitutions.

You will notice that in the definition of putc(c,f) there is a solitary \ at the end of two lines, a symbol which does not appear in the expansion of putc(). The \ is an indication to the preprocessor that the definition continues on to the next line.

●●

PROBLEM 7.4

Expand getchar() if there are the following macro definitions:

```
#define  stdin    (&_iob[0])

#define  getc(f)  (--(f)->_cnt >= 0 \
                  ? 0xff & *(f)->_ptr++ \
                  : _filbuf(f))

#define  getchar()  getc(stdin)
```

●●

▣ Discussion of problems

:::

PROBLEM 7.1

What happens if

1. There is no definition of main() in the program source code?

2. There are two definitions of main(), one in the program source code, and one in a user code file?

:::

In the discussion of these two questions, we will talk in general terms, so do not become too concerned if your C compiler system does not produce output in the form we describe. Try, as always, to grasp the ideas and concepts behind the exercise, to see how the compilation process differs on your system. Systems vary, so be wary.

First, the two queries:

1. What happens if there is no definition of main() in the program source?

```
/* C3P PROBLEM 7.1.1 program */

/* Boris Allan */

/*
 * There is no main() function
 */

#include <stdio.h>

void Fromm()
   {
   puts("An illusion\n");
   }
```

The solution to the first part of the question can be found by preparing a source code program which does not contain a definition of main(). For example, the above is a source code program which contains only one definition of a function.

When this program source is converted into object code — before the program code is linked — the process is as normal. At this stage the conversion to object code is only concerned with the grammatical form of the program (the syntax).

That is, when compiling the program to object code, the C translator is only worried about the structural rules of the language. If the final } is missing, say, then there will be a syntax error.

That there is no main() does not concern the translator, because it is quite possible that the PROBLEM 7.1.1 program is an example of a user code file, in that main() might be defined elsewhere. There is no way for the C translator to tell the difference.

It is at linking that an error is indicated. The error is that there is an unresolved external (or some similar message), where the name of the unresolved external may be _main. Frequently, a library code file name is specified as being the origin of the use of the unresolved name.

When the linker is in operation, within each object code file there may be items which are named but which are not defined.

Each variable and function used within C (such as main()) is equivalent to a code file symbol. The symbols used within the code files are usually the same as the C program source name with a preceding underline (_) and no argument list or parentheses.

The linker assumes that the definition of an undefined function is external to that file, that is, the function is defined but the definition is in another code file.

The library code assumes that there is a function main() whose definition is external to the library code file(s). In this case the definition of main() which should have occurred in the program code file. As there is no definition of main() in the program code file, the linker cannot find a definition on which to act, so therefore it cannot resolve what to do when the main() function is called.

This is why the error is indicated. The program cannot execute because there is no definition of main() (or, equivalently, no symbol _main).

2. What happens if there are two examples of main(), one in the program source, and one in a user code file?

The answer to the second part of the question is closely related to that to the first part. The difference is due mainly to the superfluity of definitions in the second case, rather than the lack of any definition of main(), as in the first case. In both cases, however, the error is not discerned until the linking takes place, because up to that stage all is legal.

The result of linking two code files, both which contain a definition of main(), is to produce an error in linking — of the form
_main symbol defined more than once (though this will vary with the system being used). The program will not execute because the linking of the code files has failed.

Again it should be emphasized: when a source code program is converted into an object code program, the C translator is only concerned with checking that the program is correctly constructed (that is, the syntax is correct).

The translator does not know whether definitions for functions, say, are given in other files, it just assumes that the definitions are so given. It is only at the linking stage of the compilation process that such checks become relevant, or possible.

PROBLEM 7.2

What happens if a function is used within the program source, but the function is not defined within any of the (standard or user) library files?

Here is a short source code program to test what happens if a nonexistent function is used within a program:

```
/* C3P PROBLEM 7.2.1 program */

/* Boris Allan */

/*
 * A nonexistent function.
 */

#include <stdio.h>

main()
    {
    puts("Before the function\n");
    aNonExistentFunction();
    puts("After the function\n");
    }
```

This program will successfully be converted into an object code program, but at the linking stage there will be an error flagged of the form that _aNonExistentFunction is an unresolved external. The location of the call to the unresolved external will be given as the program code file.

On some systems the linking will fail, and no executable code file will be produced, whereas with some linkers an executable code file will be produced. When (in the latter case) the linked code is executed, then the output will either be null (some systems) or of the form

> *Before the function*
> *After the function*

That is, the program will be executed but (when the undefined function is called) the function has a null effect.

If you are using a system which compiles, links, and then executes, it is quite possible to miss the error concerning the unresolved external, and for the incorrect operation of the program to appear a mystery. Do not go to sleep whilst the compilation process is underway, for it pays to attend to what is happening.

::

PROBLEM 7.3

What happens if a variable is used within the program source, but the variable is not declared within that source code?

::

Whereas the lack of definitions for functions is not discerned until linking, the lack of a variable declaration is not picked up until the second stage. A function is implicitly declared (without definition) merely through its use in a program — it is assumed that the definition will be provided at some stage. A variable cannot be implicitly declared in a similar manner.

Here is a short test program:

```
/* C3P PROBLEM 7.3.1 program */

/* Boris Allan */

/*
 * An undeclared variable unknownString
 */

#include <stdio.h>

main()
   {
   gets(unknownString);
   }
```

and the C translator does not get very far before it informs you that unknownstring is undefined, and stops.

Note that the program stops before any object code is produced. Not to declare a variable is a syntax error (an error in the grammatical structure), thus the translator cannot create a valid object code program.

The difference between the treatment of variables and the treatment of functions cannot be over emphasized, as the difference is based upon the distinction between translation and linking.

●●●

PROBLEM 7.4

Expand getchar() if there are the following macro definitions:

```
#define  stdin   (&_iob[0])

#define  getc(f)  (--(f)->_cnt >= 0 \
                   ? 0xff & *(f)->_ptr++ \
                   : _filbuf(f))

#define  getchar()   getc(stdin)
```

●●●

The expansion is straightforward, and does not require any knowledge of C. Here is the sequence:

1. `getchar()`
2. `getc(stdin)`
3. `getc((&_iob[0]))`
4. `(--((&_iob[0]))->_cnt >= 0`
   `? 0xff & *((&_iob[0]))->_ptr++`
   `: _filbuf((&_iob[0])))`

In the last line of the expansion we give the code on three separate lines to show its structure somewhat more clearly. It is quite possible that your system's definitions will not be at all similar to the examples given here, but the principle is the same.

In addition, the order in which the preprocessor will expand the code will not necessarily follow the sequence shown above, but the result will be the same.

At this point, I will explain the *meaning* of line 4, but start with line 1.

1.   `getchar()`

This command reads a character from the standard input stream stdin, and returns the ASCII value equivalent to that character. The command is equivalent to:

2   `getc(stdin)`

Or, `getchar()` is equivalent to a restricted form of `getc()`, where the argument to `getc()` is the standard input stream `stdin`. The meaning of `stdin` is that it is a pointer to the first element of the array of FILE structures known as `_iob[]`.

The first element is 0 (also known as the *file handle*), and so `stdin` corresponds to `_iob[0]`. As `stdin` is a pointer, we need the address of `_iob[0]`, that is, `&_iob[0]`. Thus:

3   `getc((&_iob[0]))`

The form of the `_iob[]` structure was given earlier:

```
extern struct _iobuf {
    char *_ptr;
    int   _cnt;
    char *_base;
    char _flag;
    char _file;
} _iob[20];
```

and this structure should be compared to:

4   `(--((&_iob[0]))->_cnt >= 0`
     `? 0xff & *((&_iob[0]))->_ptr++`
     `: _filbuf((&_iob[0])))`

`_cnt` is a counter, the value of which gives the number of characters left in the file. The conditional test

`--((&_iob[0]))->_cnt >= 0`

decrements the `_cnt` field of `_iob[0]` before making a test to see if the value is greater than or equal to zero.

If there are remaining characters (the test is true), then

`? 0xff & *((&_iob[0]))->_ptr++`

There are two main parts to this line.

The `*((&_iob[0]))->_ptr++` operation which produces the *content* (the initial `*`) of the character location selected (`->`) by the `_ptr` field of the pointer to the `stdin` stream (`&_iob[0]`).

The resulting character value is bitwise AND (&) with the hexadecimal value 0xff to ensure that the result is between 0 and 255. (Decimal 255 is equal to 11111111 as a binary number.)

A value preceded with 0 in C is considered to be given in octal, and a value preceded with 0x or 0X is considered to be a hexadecimal value. The value 255 (decimal) can, therefore, be any of 0377 (octal), 0xff or 0XFF (hexadecimal).

After the character is returned, the value of the pointer to characters is incremented by one unit (ptr++).

If the test produces a false result, the action is

```
_filbuf((&_iob[0])))
```

which closes the stream, resetting all pointers.

Part Three

Strings and pointers

A key to the understanding of C is the use of pointers, and pointer arithmetic. Pointer arithmetic is best shown by the topic of strings.

When one refers to the name of a string, one is (in reality) making reference to a pointer value. The pointer provides the location of the first character in the string.

Chapter 8

Strings and locations

Apart from the first chapter, we have encountered only two types of variable: the character and the integer.

When discussing nameString in earlier chapters, it was indicated that nameString only pointed to the start of a sequence of characters stored in memory. The end of the sequence was signified by the \0 (or null) character, and the declaration

```
char nameString[80];
```

set aside up to 80 successive locations for the characters to be designated by nameString.

The C system does not check to see if a particular string contains a greater number of characters than there are allocated memory locations. If the programmer is not careful, therefore, the string can overwrite unreserved locations (often causing trouble). We will start by examining what is involved in manipulating strings.

Before the examination of the first program I must reemphasize that it is very important to try out the programs, and to attempt the problems. The discussions of the solutions to the problems are an integral part of the development of the topic, and the problems enable you to begin to engage in the creative art of designing programs.

Remember that the C3P solutions are not definitive, so design new approaches for yourself, and execute your programs to establish whether your solution is appropriate.

● Strings and addresses

The following series of STRING programs is designed to illustrate the C approach to the storage of information. Before we start it is essential to reemphasize that, as far as the C language system is concerned, a string has two key characteristics:

[1] A string is described by its initial location. This means that, for example, a string identifier (that is, a string variable) is a pointer to the start of a sequence of characters which make up the string.

[2] The extent of a string is denoted by the first occurrence of a \0 (null) character in the sequence of characters which start at the given address. This means, therefore, that the C language system does not check to see if the extent of a string is less than or equal to its declared extent.

We will examine string manipulation by looking at the creation of strings, the copying of strings, and the display of strings. In the process of conducting this examination we will need to study different forms of control.

Enter, compile, and then execute, the STRING 1 program given on the next page.

```
/* C3P STRING 1 program */

/* Boris Allan */

/*
 * Use of string (character array) -
 * address and content
 */

#include <stdio.h>
```

```
main()
  {
/*
 * 10 locations for characters (in bytes)
 */
    char aStr[10], bStr[10];
    int diffAdd;
    printf("STRING 1\n\n");

/* Input strings */
    printf("First string "); fflush(stdout);
    gets(aStr);
    printf("\nSecond string "); fflush(stdout);
    gets(bStr);

/* Output address and content of each string */
    printf("\nDetails of first string:\n");
    printf("\tContent is %s\n\tAddress is %u\n",
           aStr, aStr);
    printf("\nDetails of second string:\n");
    printf("\tContent is %s\n\tAddress is %u\n",
           bStr, bStr);

/* Address calculation */
    diffAdd = (aStr > bStr
     ? aStr - bStr : bStr - aStr);
    printf("\nDifference is %u\n\n", diffAdd);
  }
```

This program sets aside storage for two strings, each of 10 characters, by use of the declaration which defines two strings as arrays of 10 characters. It should be remembered, however, that (because there has to be a null character (\0) to indicate the end of the string) each string can only contain 9 printable characters.

The two strings are known as aStr and bStr. The other name to be declared is the integer diffAdd.

There may be possible trouble with the calculation of diffAdd (that is, the difference between two pointer values). The subtraction should be admissible, though for a few C systems such a subtraction is not legal. If subtraction is not allowed, then leave out the /* Address calculation */ for the moment.

One reason why subtraction should be allowed is that the comparison

        aStr > bStr

must be admissible for all versions of C (if the version is worth the name C). A subtraction is merely an extended comparison (by how much do they differ?)

● Naming identifiers

Each identifier in the STRING 1 program is given as clear a designation as possible so that the structure and action can be more easily understood.

One adverse consequence of this verbosity is that the program is longer than needs be, if shorter names were used. For example, the conditional expression used for diffAdd

```
diffAdd = (aStr > bStr
        ? aStr - bStr : bStr - aStr);
```

could be shortened, at the expense of clarity, to
```
d = a > b ? a - b : b - a;
```

but, when we return to the program at some later stage, we will find that a great deal of work is involved in trying to establish what is happening.

It is not necessary, of course, to be quite as explicit (or as lengthy) in naming identifiers as I have so far, but it is better to err on the side of overspecification.

You will note that C3P uses a convention in which the identifier first byte vector is written firstByteVector with no spaces between words, and each new word commencing with an uppercase character.

This convention is used because firstByteVector is very readable and less subject to error in copying than, say, the use of the underline to separate words, which in this case would be first_byte_vector.

Apart from a belief that the capitalizing convention is more legible, there are two main problems with the use of the underline (some call it the *break*). First, the underline can be so light in print that it appears as a space and, second, there are possible confusions with the hyphen (especially relevant for the inexpert).

● STRING 1 in detail

The strings aStr and bStr are given a content by use of the input command gets(). This function is used because gets() is familiar – having being met in preceding chapters. In later STRING programs we will examine different ways in which strings can be given an initial content.

After the input, there is an output section during which the address of the first element of each string is printed, together with the content of the appropriate string. Study the output section in detail:

```
printf("\nDetails of first string:\n");
printf("\tContent is %s\n\tAddress is %u\n",
       aStr, aStr);
```

In the first line given here, there is a command to print out a message *Details of first string:* starting with a newline, and ending with a newline. The next printf() command is in three parts

\tContent is %s\n   Start with a tab (escape sequence \t), print out *Content is*, then print a string (format control %s), and finally move to a newline.

\tAddress is %u\n   Start with a tab (\t), print out *Address is*, then print an unsigned (positive) integer (format control %u), and finally move to a newline.

aStr, aStr   These are the content and address respectively,
                            but notice that both look exactly the same. If
                            the format instruction is %s then it is expected
                            that the corresponding item will be a pointer to
                            the start of a string (that is, aStr). If,
                            however, the format instruction is %u then it is
                            expected that the corresponding item will be a
                            positive integer (that is, aStr). A pointer is an
                            address is a positive (or, unsigned) integer.

If the address aStr is greater than the address bStr then (?)
calculate aStr − bStr else (:) calculate bStr − aStr. The result of
the calculation is assigned to the variable diffAdd. The difference
between the two addresses (aStr and bStr) is printed as a positive
integer (%u).

:::

PROBLEM 8.1

[1] The routine to produce the positive difference between two
    values is quite useful, and may quite easily be turned into a
    function which takes two arguments and produces a result to
    be assigned to a variable. Call the function diffFn(alnp, blnp).

[2] Another method by this calculation can be shortened is to
    use a #define macro (we have not examined macro
    definitions in great detail, so this will test your initiative). Call
    the macro definition diffMac(alnp, blnp).

Design both a function and a macro to calculate the positive
difference.

:::

● Allocating string locations

Here is a specimen run of the STRING 1 program:

STRING 1

First string **123456789**

Second string **abcdefghi**

Details of first string:
   Content is 123456789
   Address is 3702

Details of second string:
   Content is abcdefghi
   Address is 3692

Difference is 10

The two strings are known as aStr and bStr, and each is declared as being of 10 elements. As the final element of a string is \0 then a maximum of 9 characters may be used in each string. The value of aStr is an address, that is, the address of the first element of the string, and the same is true for bStr.

If the program is executed, the first string (aStr) is set equal to **123456789** by use of gets(), and the second string is set equal to **abcdefghi** by gets().

When aStr is printed as a string (that is, by use of the format control %s) the content of the string is output. If aStr is printed as an unsigned (positive) integer (%u) then the address of the start of the string is output. The content is *123456789* and the address is *3702*. When the action is repeated for bStr, the content is *abcdefghi* and the address is *3692*. The difference between the two addresses is *10*.

Remember that the pointer values will differ, depending upon the system in use. Some systems allocate memory in four byte chunks, and the difference between pointer addresses may have to be a multiple of four.

When aStr is declared, 10 locations are set aside, starting at 3702: when bStr is declared, 10 locations are set aside, starting at 3692. This means that — for the C system used for running STRING 1 — string pointers are stored in order in memory starting at high locations down to low.

Note that, on your system, such addresses will not be the same: indeed, string pointers may be stored in order from low to high memory locations. In later programs you will note that the pointers to strings (the addresses) will vary, partly depending upon the length of the program.

‱‱‱

PROBLEM 8.2

Here is the outcome of a run of the STRING 1 program, and the printed version of the first string is not the same as the input version. Can you explain what has happened?

STRING 1

First string **abcdefghi**

Second string **123456789012345**

Details of first string
Content is 12345
Address is 3702

Details of second string:
Content is 123456789012345
Address is 3692

Difference is 10

‱‱‱

⬤ Strings, character by character

The next program (STRING 2) takes what we have discovered from
STRING 1 and extends the program to copy the content of one string,
and store that content in a new string.

The first real difference in this program is the initialization of
indexStr to 0 in the declaration. The second difference is that only
the first string (aStr) is input by use of gets(), and bStr is copied
from aStr by use of a do–loop.

There is no provision in C for a string to be treated as a complete
entity: when we refer to the string by name (for example, aStr or
bStr), we are only referring to the first location of the string. To refer
to the content of the first element of the string, we use aStr[0] or
bStr[0] (or, alternatively *aStr or *bStr). In the case of
structures or unions, the name refers to a pointer to the first
location of the construct.

To make a copy of a string, therefore, we have to copy each single
character: thus to copy the fifth character of aStr to the fifth
character of bStr we assign

```
bStr[4] = aStr[4];
```

and if (in general) we index each successive location by the identifier
indexStr, we copy by

```
bStr[indexStr] = aStr[indexStr];
```

increasing the value of indexStr by a unit at a time.

We continue to copy characters up to and including the \0 (null
character) terminator, and then stop. This is the action of the routine
in the program:

```
do
    bStr[indexStr] = aStr[indexStr];
while (aStr[indexStr++] != '\0');
```

which means that the loop executes while the character just copied is
not the null character.

The program:

```
/* C3P STRING 2 program */

/* Boris Allan */

/*
 * Use of string, and making a copy.
 */

#include <stdio.h>

main()
    {
    char aStr[10], bStr[10];
    int diffAdd, indexStr = 0;
    printf("STRING 2\n\n");
    printf("First string "); fflush(stdout);
    gets(aStr);
/*
 * Copy aStr to bStr character by character
 */
    do
        bStr[indexStr] = aStr[indexStr];
    while (aStr[indexStr++] != '\0');
    printf("\nDetails of first string:\n");
    printf("\tContent is %s\n\tAddress is %u\n",
        aStr, aStr);
    printf("\nDetails of second string:\n");
    printf("\tContent is %s\n\tAddress is %u\n",
        bStr, bStr);
    diffAdd = (aStr > bStr
        ? aStr - bStr : bStr - aStr);
    printf("\nDifference is %u\n\n", diffAdd);
    }
```

The do–loop always executes once, so that the first element of aStr is always copied to the first element of bStr. In other languages the while might be replaced by an until, and by use of the macro substitution

```
#define until while !
```

it is possible to rewrite the routine as

```
do
    bStr[indexStr] = aStr[indexStr];
until (aStr[indexStr++] == '\0');
```

That is, perform the action designated in the do section (that is, copy a character), until the character aStr[indexStr] is equal to \0, or while ! (not) equal to \0.

The ++ operator means that when the test is complete the value of indexStr is incremented by one unit, and so the do section operates on the next element of the string. The do–loop shows how neatly it is possible to manipulate data in C.

Here is an example session, and note in particular that the addresses of aStr and bStr are different from those in the program STRING 1:

STRING 2

First string **abcdef**

Details of first string:
Content is abcdef
Address is 3684

Details of second string:
Content is abcdef
Address is 3674

Difference is 10

Why is there a difference in the start addresses of the strings — compared to the earlier program?

■ Discussion of problems

:::

PROBLEM 8.1

[1] The routine to produce the positive difference between two values is quite useful, and may quite easily be turned into a function which takes two arguments and produces a result to be assigned to a variable. Call the function diffFn(alnp, blnp).

[2] Another method by this calculation can be shortened is to use a #define macro (we have not examined macro definitions in great detail, so this will test your initiative). Call the macro definition diffMac(alnp, blnp).

Design both a function and a macro to calculate the positive difference.

:::

A program to illustrate the `diffFn()` is not difficult to construct, and one example is given on the next page.

```
/* C3P PROBLEM 8.1.1 program */

/* Boris Allan */

/*
 * Positive difference between
 * two integers: function version
 */

#include <stdio.h>

main()
    {
    int smallInt = 3, bigInt = 25,
        diffInt;
    diffInt = diffFn(smallInt,bigInt);
    printf("Difference is %d\n\n", diffInt);

    diffInt = diffFn(bigInt,smallInt);
    printf("Difference is %d\n\n", diffInt);
    }

diffFn(aInp,bInp)
int aInp, bInp;
    {
    return (aInp > bInp
            ? aInp - bInp : bInp - aInp);
    }
```

I have not declared diffFn() in the main() function, because
diffFn() returns an integer (the default type).

Concentrating on the definition of the diffFn() function: there
are two arguments (both of which are integers), and the content of the
definition is return the (? :) conditional expression we met in
STRING 1. The command return means that the value returned by
the function is calculated as either aInp - bInp or bInp - aInp —
depending on which is the larger.

The result of executing the program is

Difference is 22

Difference is 22

which shows that the positive difference is returned by the function.

The macro definition produces a different style of program, and is accomplished by placing the #define before the main() function:

```
/* C3P PROBLEM 8.1.2 program */

/* Boris Allan */

/*
 * Positive difference between
 * two integers: macro version
 */

#include <stdio.h>

#define diffMac(aInp,bInp) \
      (aInp > bInp \
       ? aInp - bInp : bInp - aInp)

main()
   {
   int smallInt = 3, bigInt = 25,
         diffInt;
   diffInt = diffMac(smallInt,bigInt);
   printf("Difference is %d\n\n", diffInt);

   diffInt = diffMac(bigInt,smallInt);
   printf("Difference is %d\n\n", diffInt);
   }
```

Note that in the macro definition, each line (other than the last) ends with the \ symbol, which means that the definition continues on to the next line. The reason the definition is split in this manner is to try to emphasize the similarity of the structure of the macro to the original form in STRING 1.

The PROBLEM 8.1.2 program, when expanded by the preprocessor, produces a C source given below. Note that I have rearranged the format of the conditional to match that in STRING 1 — in the original preprocessor listing the conditional was all on one long line.

```
main()
   {
int smallInt = 3, bigInt - 25,
       diffInt;
diffInt = (smallInt > bigInt
       ? smallInt - bigInt : bigInt - smallInt);
printf("Difference is %d\n\n", diffInt);

diffInt = (bigInt > smallInt
       ? bigInt - smallInt : smallInt - bigInt);
printf("Difference is %d\n\n", diffInt);
   }
```

After preprocessing the PROBLEM 8.1.1 program, the diffFn() call still remains intact. It is only with the macro definition diffMac() in PROBLEM 8.1.2 that replacement takes place. The output from the PROBLEM 8.1.2 program is exactly the same as that from PROBLEM 8.1.1.

We have, therefore, two methods of achieving the same result: the function definition or the macro definition. It is worth discussing which of the two approaches is preferable in specific instances, and which is preferable in general.

Here are certain points to help in your discussion, and you may add your own points to the list.

☐ With a macro definition the program commands are inserted into the source, and are executed directly, with two consequences:

    ☐ Execution is swifter with the macro definition, because there are no overheads due to function calls.

    □   If there are many calls to the macro facility then, as the code is expanded at each call to the definition, it is possible that the source program can become too long.

  □ It is not feasible to code complex sequences of commands as macro definitions, and the content of the macro definition is not protected from the rest of the program in the way that the content of a function definition is protected. Function definitions are inherently more secure than macro definitions.

For the above example, there is much to be said in favour of the diffMac() definition because the content is short and does not affect any variable other than those given as arguments.

::

PROBLEM 8.2

Here is the outcome of a run of the STRING 1 program, and the printed version of the first string is not the same as the input version. Can you explain what has happened?

STRING 1

First string **abcdefghi**

Second string **123456789012345**

Details of first string
Content is 12345
Address is 3702

Details of second string:
Content is 123456789012345
Address is 3692

Difference is 10

::

The first string (aStr) is stored in locations 3702 to 3711, and thus, when the first string is input, the locations are occupied as follows

LOCATION CHAR

LOCATION	CHAR	
3702	a	aStr
3703	b	
3704	c	
3705	d	
3706	e	
3707	f	
3708	g	
3709	h	
3710	i	
3711	\0	

The second string (bStr) starts at location 3692, and has memory set aside up to location 3701. If the second string extends beyond 10 locations, the bStr intrudes into memory set aside for aStr. That is,

LOCATION	CHAR	
3692	1	bStr
3693	2	
3694	3	
3695	4	
3696	5	
3697	6	
3698	7	
3699	8	
3700	9	
3701	0	
3702	1	aStr
3703	2	
3704	3	
3705	4	
3706	5	
3707	\0	

3708	g
3709	h
3710	i
3711	\0

What has happened is that the second string (bStr) has overwritten part of the first string (aStr). When the first string is printed, the printf() function considers the string to start at location 3702 and continue until the first occurrence of a \0 character.

Location 3702 now — after being overwritten — contains the 1 character, and the first occurrence of \0 is at location 3707: thus the string is considered to be 12345.

When the second string (bStr) is printed, the string is considered to start at location 3692, and to continue up to the first \0 (at location 3707) – thus aStr and bStr overlap.

If the storage of strings on your system is in a different order, then the output will probably differ, so take care.

Chapter 9

Strings and pointers

We have seen how the allocation of memory is crucial to the understanding of the operation of strings in C.

An understanding of memory allocation is one of the keys to understanding C, and we are using the analysis of strings to help in a general study of memory in C.

The construction of functions is taken further in the discussion of problems.

● Character by character

The next program (STRING 3) takes the notion of character by character access to a string further by printing out each string character by character:

```
/* C3P STRING 3 program */

/* Boris Allan */

/*
 * Use of string (character array),
 * making a copy of the string, and
 * printing out both strings using
 * the basic putchar() function
 */
```

```
#include <stdio.h>

main()
    {
    char aStr[10], bStr[10];
    int diffAdd, indexStr = 0;
    printf("STRING 3\n\n");
    printf("First string "); fflush(stdout);
    gets(aStr);
    do
        bStr[indexStr] = aStr[indexStr];
    while (aStr[indexStr++] != '\0');

    printf("\nDetails of first string:\n");
    printf("\tContent is ");
    for (indexStr = 0;
            aStr[indexStr] != '\0'; indexStr++)
        putchar(aStr[indexStr]);
    printf("\n\tAddress is %u\n", aStr);

    printf("\nDetails of second string:\n");
    printf("\tContent is ");
    for (indexStr = 0;
            bStr[indexStr] != '\0'; indexStr++)
        putchar(bStr[indexStr]);
    printf("\n\tAddress is %u\n", bStr);

    diffAdd = (aStr > bStr
            ? aStr - bStr : bStr - aStr);
    printf("\nDifference is %u\n\n", diffAdd);
    }
```

The new routine in this program is that to print out the content of a
string, character by character, that is (with comments):

```
for (indexStr = 0;                    /* 1 */
        aStr[indexStr] != '\0';       /* 2 */
        indexStr++)                   /* 3 */
     putchar(aStr[indexStr]);
```

which uses a for-loop to step through the characters in the string until the \0 character is encountered. The three parts of the for-loop have the following actions:

[1] The integer indexStr is set to zero.

[2] The character indicated by aStr[indexStr] is compared with the null character \0, and if the character is not \0 then the body of the for-loop is executed.

[3] At the end of each pass through the for-loop (each iteration) the value of indexStr is incremented by one unit.

The body of the for-loop is simply

```
putchar(aStr[indexStr])
```

which is a command to put the character at aStr[indexStr] on the standard output stream (usually, this prints the character on the screen).

Here is specimen printed text from the above program

STRING 3

First string **3456789**

Details of first string:
    Content is 3456789
    Address is 3664

Details of second string:
    Content is 3456789
    Address is 3674

Difference is 10

Which is the same form of output as the previous program.

● Pointers and content

The STRING 4 program is designed to illustrate the consequences of an equivalence. The equivalence is that

aStr[0] IS EQUIVALENT TO *aStr

aStr[1] IS EQUIVALENT TO *(aStr + 1)

and so forth. That is:

☐ aStr denotes the value of the address at which the sequence of characters known by the name aStr commences;

☐ aStr[0] denotes the value stored at the location whose address is aStr (that is, address (aStr + 0));

☐ *aStr (or, *(aStr + 0)) denotes the value stored at the location whose address is aStr — the monadic (pointer) operator * is not to be confused with the dyadic (multiplicative) operator *;

☐ aStr[1] denotes the value stored at the location whose address is (aStr + 1);

☐ *(aStr + 1) denotes the value stored at the location whose address is aStr + 1.

IMPORTANT. Note that *(aStr + aValue) is not the same as *aStr + aValue, but that *aStr++ is the same as *(aStr++) and not the same as (*aStr)++. It is as well in any case to use parentheses to make the meaning clear.

PROBLEM 9.1

[1] Design at least two different functions to print a string, so that (for example) to print aStr you use the call printString(aStr).

[2] Why is the use of a macro definition not as suitable as is the use of a function definition?

🌑 Printing strings

Here is the program:

```
/* C3P STRING 4 program */

/* Boris Allan */

/*
 * Print out the address for each element of
 * the string, and the content as a character
 */
```

```
#include <stdio.h>

/* Adds slight generality */
#define STRSIZE 10

main()
    {
    char aStr[STRSIZE], bStr[STRSIZE];
    int diffAdd, indexStr = 0;
    printf("STRING 4\n\nFirst string ");
    fflush(stdout); gets(aStr);

    do
        *(bStr + indexStr) = *(aStr + indexStr);
    while (*(aStr + indexStr++) != '\0');

    printf("\nDetails of first string:\n");
    printf("\tContent is ");
    for (indexStr = 0;
            *(aStr + indexStr) != '\0';
            indexStr++)
        putchar(*(aStr + indexStr));
    printf("\n\tAddress is %u\n", aStr);

    printf("\nDetails of second string:\n");
    printf("\tContent is ");
    for (indexStr = 0;
            bStr[indexStr] != '\0';
            indexStr++)
        putchar(bStr[indexStr]);
    printf("\n\tAddress is %u\n", bStr);
    diffAdd = (aStr > bStr
            ? aStr - bStr : bStr - aStr);
    printf("\nDifference is %u\n\n", diffAdd);
```

```
/* Print location, and content as a character */
   printf("First string\n\n");
   for (indexStr = 0;
        indexStr <= STRSIZE - 1;
        indexStr++)
      printf("%u    %c\n",
             aStr + indexStr, *(aStr + indexStr));
   printf("\n\nSecond string\n\n");
   for (indexStr = 0;
        indexStr <= STRSIZE - 1;
        indexStr++)
      printf("%u    %c\n",
             bStr + indexStr, *(bStr + indexStr));
}
```

The STRING 4 program has several changes from the previous
(STRING 3) program, and the purpose of the

```
#define STRSIZE 10
```

directive is to increase generality. The first important distinction is the
change from

```
do
    bStr[indexStr] = aStr[indexStr];
while (aStr[indexStr++] != '\0');
```

in STRING 3 to the equivalent

```
do
    *(bStr + indexStr) = *(aStr + indexStr);
while (*(aStr + indexStr++) != '\0');
```

in STRING 4. At this point it might be worth returning to the
PROBLEM 9.1.2 program and reexamining the bPrtStr() function.
The equivalences are exact, because (for example)
aStr[indexStr++] means exactly the same as
*(aStr + indexStr++).

Within the STRING 4 program the two routines

```
for (indexStr = 0;
        *(aStr + indexStr) != '\0';
        indexStr++)
    putchar(*(aStr + indexStr));


    . . . . . . . . . . .


for (indexStr = 0;
        bStr[indexStr] != '\0';
        indexStr++)
    putchar(bStr[indexStr]);
```

have exactly the same effect, except that the first prints the content of
aStr, and the second prints the content of bStr. Study the
equivalences.

The two final routines print out the address of a location, and the
content of that location expressed as a character. The body of the
for–loop is

```
printf("%u    %c\n",
        aStr + indexStr, *(aStr + indexStr));
```

That is, print a positive (unsigned, %u) integer, and print a character
(%c) on the same line, then move to a newline (\n). The unsigned
integer is the address of a location (that is, aStr + indexStr), and
the character is the content of that same location (that is,
*(aStr + indexStr)). It is possible to output the content of the
location in many other different forms, and this will be shown in
program STRING 4.1.

Here is example output from STRING 4:

STRING 4

First string **abcdefghi**

Details of first string:
    Content is abcdefghi
    Address is 3732

Details of second string:
    Content is abcdefghi
    Address is 3722

Difference is 10

First string

3732   a
3733   b
3734   c
3735   d
3736   e
3737   f
3738   g
3739   h
3740   i
3741

Second string

3722	a
3723	b
3724	c
3725	d
3726	e
3727	f
3728	g
3729	h
3730	i
3731	

This output should be compared with the structure of the STRING 4 program, and it should be noted that the address for both strings differs from previous values.

::

PROBLEM 9.2

Design a function to print a string, character by character, alongside the address of the location in which that character is stored.

::

● Character values

The program STRING 4.1 is exactly the same as STRING 4, except
for this section:

```
/*
 *. STRING 4.1 modification to STRING 4
 * STRING 4 is unaltered save the following.
 *
 * Print location, and content in decimal.
 */
printf("First string\n\n");
for (indexStr = 0;
     indexStr <= STRSIZE - 1;
     indexStr++)
/*
 * %d (signed decimal integer) not
 * %c (character) in printf()
 */
    printf("%d   %d\n",
        aStr + indexStr, *(aStr + indexStr));

printf("\n\nSecond string\n\n");
for (indexStr = 0;
     indexStr <= STRSIZE - 1;
     indexStr++)
    printf("%d   %d\n",
        bStr + indexStr, *(bStr + indexStr));
```

Here an example output from STRING 4.1:

STRING 4.1

First string **abcdefghi**

Details of first string:
Content is abcdefghi
Address is 3748

Details of second string:
Content is abcdefghi
Address is 3738

Difference is 10

First string

3748	97
3749	98
3750	99
3751	100
3752	101
3753	102
3754	103
3755	104
3756	105
3757	0

Second string

3738	97
3739	98
3740	99
3741	100
3742	101
3743	102
3744	103
3745	104
3746	105
3747	0

The ASCII value for the character a is 97, which means that when stored in a location (a byte, or 8 bits), the character is stored as a number whose value is 97.

ASCII (American Standard Code for Information Interchange) is the normal means by which character (or textual) information is stored in many other languages, as well as C.

If the ASCII value for a is 97, as has been noted, the ASCII value for i (the last character in the string) is 105. The ASCII value corresponding to \0 is thus 0: to find the end of a string the system searches for the first occurrence of the value 0.

C always treats a character as an ASCII value, and all comparisons are of values, not of the characters themselves. The %c format instruction means that the ASCII value (any value in fact) is converted to the appropriate ASCII character on output.

On some C systems characters can take values from 0 to 255 (though only values from 0 to 127 are defined in the ASCII standard), whereas for other systems the values taken by a character can range from −128 to 127. This is the distinction between unsigned character values (0 to 255) and signed character values (−128 to 127) which has correspondences to unsigned and signed integers.

In the signed representation of characters −1 is equivalent to the unsigned value 255, because −1 + 1 = 0, and 255 + 1 = 256 = 0 for an 8 bit byte. One way to find whether your C system uses signed or unsigned characters is to run STRING 4.1, but with a string of fewer than nine elements:

STRING 4.1

First string **abcd**

Details of first string:
  Content is abcd
  Address is 3748

Details of second string:
  Content is abcd
  Address is 3738

Difference is 10

First string

3748   97
3749   98
3750   99
3751   100
3752   0
3753   −1
3754   −47
3755   −29
3756   −47
3757   −29

Second string

3738	97
3739	98
3740	99
3741	100
3742	0
3743	15
3744	−96
3745	2
3746	12
3747	0

and, as can be seen, the C system used for this program uses signed characters.

The string abcd is only four characters long, plus the \0 stored at 3741 and 3751, thus the other locations are filled with random rubbish, and have not been explicitly loaded with any value. Each run of this program, even with the same string on the same system, will probably produce different values. Your system will certainly be completely different in the values output in the unfilled locations and, indeed, your system might use unsigned characters.

■ Discussion of problems

:::

PROBLEM 9.1

[1] Design at least two different functions to print a string, so that (for example) to print aStr you use the call printString(aStr).

[2] Why is the use of a macro definition not as suitable as is the use of a function definition?

:::

We will call the two alternative functions aPrtStr() and bPrtStr(). In aPrtStr() we will use a local variable (indexStr) to step through the locations starting at stringPtr, using a while-loop to check for the end of the string.

```
/* C3P PROBLEM 9.1.1 program */

/* Boris Allan */

/*
 * Print a string, first version is aPrtStr()
 */
```

```
#include <stdio.h>

main()
    {
    char exampleStr[10];
    void aPrtStr(char *);

    gets(exampleStr);    printf("String is ");
    aPrtStr(exampleStr);
    putchar('\n');
    }

void aPrtStr(stringPtr)
char stringPtr[];
    {
    int indexStr = 0;
    while (stringPtr[indexStr] != '\0')
        putchar(stringPtr[indexStr++]);
    }
```

The function takes one argument, stringPtr, which is declared as a
pointer to the start of a sequence of characters (stringPtr[]). The
local integer variable indexStr is initialized to 0, and the while-loop
executes while the content of stringPtr[indexStr] is not equal to
\0. Effectively, stringPtr[indexStr] is a pointer to a location
whose content is assumed to be a character. I will leave you to
establish the operation of the body of the while-loop, that is,

```
putchar(stringPtr[indexStr++])
```

but by now you should have no difficulty in disentangling the sense.
This function works perfectly well, but the next version has even more
of the flavour of C.

Here is the bPrtStr() function, with a main() program which
uses bPrtStr() — identical to the previous main() apart from the
name of the function called.

```
/* C3P PROBLEM 9.1.2 program */

/* Boris Allan */

/*
 * Print a string, second version is bPrtStr()
 */

#include <stdio.h>

main()
    {
    char exampleStr[10];
    void bPrtStr(char *);

    gets(exampleStr);

    printf("String is ");
    bPrtStr(exampleStr);
    putchar('\n');
    }

void bPrtStr(stringPtr)
char stringPtr[];
    {
    while (stringPtr[0] != '\0')
        putchar(stringPtr++[0]);
    }
```

The argument stringPtr is, as has been already noted, a pointer to
the start of a string (a sequence of characters). We have seen it is
possible to start at different points along a string.

The bPrtStr() function checks to see if the first element of the
string (stringPtr[0]) is equivalent to the null character (\0). While
the character is not null, the character is printed and then the pointer
is incremented by one unit (stringPtr++) [1].

As the argument is only passed by value and the C translator does not remember the name of the variable used in the call, incrementing stringPtr has no effect on the value of exampleStr in the main() function — or any other function.

The reason why a macro definition does not make sense in this case is that (as values are incremented) changes will be made in the content of variables in main(), and thus the use of the routine would not be secure.

●●

PROBLEM 9.2

Design a function to print a string, character by character, alongside the address of the location in which that character is stored.

●●

In effect, this problem requires a function to emulate the action of the replicated routine in the STRING 4 program, that is,

```
printf("First string\n\n");
for (indexStr - 0; indexStr <= STRSIZE - 1;
     indexStr++)
   printf("%u    %c\n",
          aStr + indexStr, *(aStr + indexStr));
```

As always, we want to achieve more generality — otherwise why bother with a function?

To this end, therefore, a function which has two inputs (that is, two arguments or parameters). The first argument is the start of the sequence of characters, and the second argument is the length of the string that we wish to print. The length of the string may be more or less than the real length of the string, but the printing does not cease when a \0 is encountered.

The length of the string will be an integer, but the address of the string will be a pointer: though addresses and integers are both numbers, they are numbers with different interpretations, as indicated by program PROBLEM 9.2.1,

```
/* C3P PROBLEM 9.2.1 program */

/* Boris Allan */

/*
 * Print characters with the address
 * first version
 */

#include <stdio.h>

main()
    {
    char exampleStr[10];
    void aListChars(char *, unsigned);

    gets(exampleStr);
    printf("String\n\n");
    aListChars(exampleStr, 10);
    }

void aListChars(inStr, lenStr)
char *inStr;          /* string pointer */
unsigned lenStr;      /* string length */
    {
/*
 * The address is treated as an  integer,
 * but there are warnings about levels of
 * 'indirection' at commented lines
 */
    for (lenStr += inStr - 1 ;     /* */
          inStr <= lenStr;         /* */
          inStr++)
       printf("%u  %c\n", inStr, *inStr);
    }
```

The address of the start of the input string is inStr (a pointer to a sequence of characters), and the length of the string is lenStr. The length is converted to the address of the final location of the string, by

```
lenStr = lenStr + inStr - 1;
```

an assignment which can be simplified by the C operator +=

```
lenStr += inStr - 1;
```

It has to be remembered, however, that lenStr and inStr are of different types, one is a pointer and one is a positive integer. inStr points to a location, and lenStr gives the value in a location. Though both have positive integer values their natures differ.

With some languages it is not possible to mix numbers whose types differ, but C will allow this mixing, though (in this case) most C translators will signal a warning. The C system used to compile this program puts a warning that the line

```
lenStr += inStr - 1;
```

has *different levels of indirection*. Indirection is the term used to describe the ability in C to find a value indirectly through its address. (This why the assignment line has the empty comment /* */.)

The line

```
inStr <= lenStr;
```

compares two quantities at different levels of indirection (that is, a pointer to a character and an unsigned integer), and the C translator establishes there is a difference in status.

In the case of this program, we want to mix values in this way, but the warnings are there to help if we have unknowingly mixed our values. Many other mixes do not produce warnings, but mixing different levels of indirection is sufficiently important (and easy to discern) that warnings are normally given with most C systems.

In a sense, we should try to make explicit what it is we are attempting to perform, because at some later time we may wonder what we have been doing in confusing the levels of indirection. The next program tries to make explicit the planned action: the effect of this program is exactly the same, but this time there are no warnings — we have clarified the status of each variable.

```
/* C3P PROBLEM 9.2.2 program */

/* Boris Allan */

/*
 * Print characters with the address,
 * second version
 */

#include <stdio.h>

main()
    {
    char exampleStr[10];
    void bListChars(char *, unsigned);

    gets(exampleStr);

    printf("String\n\n");
    bListChars(exampleStr, 10);
    }

void bListChars(inStr, lenStr)
char *inStr;
unsigned lenStr;
    {
/*
 * The address inStr is 'cast' as
 * an unsigned integer
 */
    for (lenStr += (unsigned) (inStr - 1);
            (unsigned) inStr <= lenStr;
            inStr++)
        printf("%u  %c\n", inStr, *inStr);
    }
```

This time the function (bListChars()) uses a facility to cast a value to an appropriate type. When the pointer is used in conjunction with the unsigned integer, the pointer is cast to appear as an unsigned integer by prefixing the pointer name with the type to which it is to be cast (enclosed in parentheses).

Thus (for example) the line

```
lenStr += (unsigned) (inStr - 1);
```

takes the pointer value less one unit (that is, (inStr - 1)), treats the result as an entity — due to the parentheses — and considers the resulting pointer value as an unsigned integer, which is then added to lenStr.

Even though the first version of the function operates successfully, the cast commands help in understanding the operation of the second version of the function.

The preceding two functions are terrible. They have taken a bad idea (converting a pointer to an unsigned integer), and have tried to make the best of that bad idea. In effect, we have tried to treat C as if it were any ordinary language, and C is not ordinary. Here is a much better function:

```
void cListChars(inStr, lenStr)
char *inStr;
unsigned lenStr;
    {
    char *endStr = inStr + lenStr - 1;
    do
        printf("%u %c\n", inStr, *inStr);
    while (inStr++ != endStr);
    }
```

No problems with indirection, no need to cast. The complete program (without comments) is

```
#include <stdio.h>

main()
    {
    char exampleStr[10];
    void cListChars(char *, unsigned);
    gets(exampleStr);
    printf("String\n\n");
    cListChars(exampleStr, 10);
    }

void cListChars(inStr, lenStr)
char *inStr;
unsigned lenStr;
    {
    char *endStr = inStr + lenStr - 1;
    do
        printf("%u %c\n", inStr, *inStr);
    while (inStr++ != endStr);
    }
```

I leave you to disentangle the workings of this program.

Note

[1]   A neater while–loop is

```
while (*stringPtr != '\0')
    putchar(*stringPtr++);
```

but this will have to wait until we have examined the explicit use of pointers.

Chapter 10

Strings and functions

In this chapter we will investigate in more detail the ways in which one can copy the content of one string to another, and discover where and how strings are stored in memory.

In addition, various consequences of the use of strings with a function are examined, with the aim of revealing more about both strings and functions. There are no problems in this chapter.

● Copying strings

Rather than copying the content of aStr to bStr by two separate sections of code within the program, it is possible to use a function copyString().

Before we go further, remember that it is only possible to pass over a value as an argument to a function. The C system keeps no track of the name of the item used as argument, and modifications in the value within a function are not reflected in the variable in the calling function.

In the case of a string identifier, we pass the address of the string to a function, and that is all.

The first example program is STRING 5, a program that uses a do–loop to control the action of the function copyString(). The elements of the string are selected by indirection, and the character arrays destinationString and sourceString are indexed by the local variable indxStr. You should compare the function to the equivalent code in STRING 4.

```
/* C3P STRING 5 program */

/* Boris Allan */

/*
 * Copying a string by use of copyString()
 */

#include <stdio.h>
#define STR 10

main()
    {
    void copyString(char *, char *);
    char aStr[STR], bStr[STR];
    int diffAdd, indxStr = 0;

    printf("STRING 5\n\n");
    printf("First string "); fflush(stdout);
    gets(aStr);

/* New function to copy strings */
    copyString(aStr, bStr);
    printf("\nDetails of first string:\n");
    printf("\tContent is %s\n\tAddress is %u\n",
        aStr, aStr);
    printf("\nDetails of second string:\n");
    printf("\tContent is %s\n\tAddress is %u\n",
        bStr, bStr);

    diffAdd = (aStr > bStr
        ? aStr - bStr : bStr - aStr);
    printf("\nAddress difference is %u\n\n",
        diffAdd);
```

```
    printf("First string\n\n");
    for (indxStr = 0; indxStr <= STR - 1;
         indxStr++)
       printf("%u    %c\n", aStr + indxStr,
            *(aStr + indxStr));
    printf("\n\nSecond string\n\n");
    for (indxStr = 0; indxStr <= STR - 1;
         indxStr++)
       printf("%u    %c\n", bStr + indxStr,
            *(bStr + indxStr));
    }

void copyString(srcStr, destStr)
/*
 * Function to copy srcStr to destStr:
 * note the two forms of declaration (*srcStr,
 * destStr[]) both of which are equivalent.
 */
char *srcStr, destStr[];
    {
    int indxStr = 0;
/*
 * There are alternative forms of
 * presenting the manipulation of
 * strings in this do-loop
 */
    do
       destStr[indxStr] = srcStr[indxStr];
    while (srcStr[indxStr++] != '\0');
    }
```

The program (without comments) looks like this:

```
#include <stdio.h>
#define STR 10

main()
    {
    void copyString(char *, char *);
    char aStr[STR], bStr[STR];
    int diffAdd, indxStr = 0;

    printf("STRING 5\n\n");
    printf("First string "); fflush(stdout);
    gets(aStr);
    copyString(aStr, bStr);
    printf("\nDetails of first string:\n");
    printf("\tContent is %s\n\tAddress is %u\n",
            aStr, aStr);
    printf("\nDetails of second string:\n");
    printf("\tContent is %s\n\tAddress is %u\n",
            bStr, bStr);
    diffAdd = (aStr > bStr
            ? aStr - bStr : bStr - aStr);
    printf("\nAddress difference is %u\n\n",
            diffAdd);

    printf("First string\n\n");
    for (indxStr = 0; indxStr <= STR - 1;
            indxStr++)
        printf("%u    %c\n", aStr + indxStr,
                *(aStr + indxStr));
    printf("\n\nSecond string\n\n");
    for (indxStr = 0; indxStr <= STR - 1;
            indxStr++)
        printf("%u    %c\n", bStr + indxStr,
                *(bStr + indxStr));
    }
```

```
void copyString(srcStr, destStr)
char *srcStr, destStr[];
    {
    int indxStr = 0;

    do
        destStr[indxStr] = srcStr[indxStr];
    while (srcStr[indxStr++] != '\0');
    }
```

⬤ Comments : an aside

At this point, the content of the copyString() function may not be too clear because of the commenting: note that the bones of the function may be perceived in the skeletal form we will call cpyStr().

```
void cpyStr(src, dst)
char *src, *dst;
    {
    int i = 0;
    do dst[i] - src[i];
    while (src[i++] != '\0');
    }
```

The action of copyString() and of cpyStr() are identical. In some senses the definition as given in cpystr() is preferable to that of copyString(), because of the extreme commenting in STRING 5.

The definition (of cpyStr()) is preferable because it is shorter, and — for experienced C programmers — there is no need to comment quite as extensively as for the copyString() function. The point is, however, that when learning C it is as well to be verbose in one's commenting and naming because of the help this gives in understanding the program. Even so, experienced programmers quite often omit comments and do not give helpful names — to their later confusion.

Here is printed output from the above program:

STRING 5

First string **qwertyuio**

Details of first string:
    Content is qwertyuio
    Address is 3732

Details of second string:
    Content is qwertyuio
    Address is 3722

Address difference is 10

First string

3732   q
3733   w
3734   e
3735   r
3736   t
3737   y
3738   u
3739   i
3740   o
3741

Second string

3722 q
3723 w
3724 e
3725 r
3726 t
3727 y
3728 u
3729 i
3730 o
3731

This is the STRING 5.1 program:

```
#include <stdio.h>
#define S 10
main() { void cs(char *, char *);
char a[S], b[S]; int d, i = 0;
printf("STRING 5.1\n\nFirst string ");
fflush(stdout); gets(a); cs(a, b);
printf("\nDetails of first string:\n");
printf("\tContent is %s\n\tAddress is %u\n", a, a);
printf("\nDetails of second string:\n");
printf("\tContent is %s\n\tAddress is %u\n", b, b);
d = (a > b ? a - b : b - a);
printf("\nAddress difference is %u\n\n", d);
printf("First string\n\n");
for (i = 0; i <= S - 1; i++)
printf("%u %c\n", a + i, *(a + i));
printf("\n\nSecond string\n\n");
for (i = 0; i <= S - 1; i++)
printf("%u %c\n", b + i, *(b + i)); }
void cs(s, d) char *s, *d; {
int i = 0; do d[i] = s[i];
while (s[i++] != '\0'); }
```

The operation of the simplified program is almost impossible to discern, even for the expert, so remember to think about the readability of programs you write. Note that the action is the same, for here is comparable output:

STRING 5.1

First string **qwertyuio**

Details of first string:
   Content is qwertyuio
   Address is 3746

Details of second string:
   Content is qwertyuio
   Address is 3736

Address difference is 10

First string

3746 q
3747 w
3748 e
3749 r
3750 t
3751 y
3752 u
3753 i
3754 o
3755

Second string

3736 q
3737 w
3738 e
3739 r
3740 t
3741 y
3742 u
3743 i
3744 o
3745

The only notable differences between the results of executing STRING 5 and STRING 5.1 are the locations of the start of the strings. Such differences in the addresses are due to different lengths of the programs.

Before it appears as if I am suggesting that verbose commenting is essential, it is worth recognizing that (in many respects) comments are only necessary to highlight notable instances.

If the algorithms used are standard, for example, then helpful names and a consistent form of presentation of the program means that programs can often be self-documenting. The program STRING 5.2 attempts to illustrate this feature:

```
/* C3P STRING 5.2 program */

/* Boris Allan */

#include <stdio.h>
#define STRINGSIZE 10

main()
   {
   void copyString(char *, char *);
   char aString[STRINGSIZE],
         bString[STRINGSIZE];
   int diffAddress, indexString = 0;
   printf("STRING 5.2\n\n");
   printf("First string "); fflush(stdout);
   gets(aString);

   copyString(aString, bString);

   printf("\nDetails of first string:\n");
   printf("\tContent is %s\n\tAddress is %u\n",
         aString, aString);
   printf("\nDetails of second string:\n");
   printf("\tContent is %s\n\tAddress is %u\n",
         bString, bString);
   diffAddress = (aString > bString
         ? aString - bString : bString - aString);
   printf("\nAddress difference is %u\n\n",
         diffAddress);
```

```
    printf("First string\n\n");
    for (indexString = 0;
            indexString <= STRINGSIZE - 1;
            indexString++)
        printf("%u    %c\n", aString + indexString,
                *(aString + indexString));
    printf("\n\nSecond string\n\n");
    for (indexString = 0;
            indexString <= STRINGSIZE - 1;
            indexString++)
        printf("%u    %c\n", bString + indexString,
                *(bString + indexString));
    }


void copyString(sourceString,
        destString)
char *sourceString, destString[];
    {
    int indexString - 0;
    do
        destString[indexString]
            = sourceString[indexString];
    while (sourceString[indexString++] != '\0');
    }
```

I would suggest that STRING 5.2 is an easy program to follow
because of the extensive use of meaningful names, the constructive use
of blank lines, and a consistent method of illustrating control by use of
indentation.

● Investigating the copying of strings

The three final versions of this task are designed to illustrate various aspects of string manipulation as shown in the copying of strings. The first program is:

```
/* C3P STRING 6 program */

/* Boris Allan */

/*
 * Copying a string by use of
 * a general function known as
 * copyString() - second version
 */

#include <stdio.h>
#define SIZE 10

main()
    {
    void copyString(char *, char *);
    char aStr[SIZE], bStr[SIZE];
    int diffAddress, indexStr = 0;

    printf("STRING 6\n\nFirst string ");
    fflush(stdout); gets(aStr);
    copyString(aStr, bStr);
    printf("\nDetails of first string:\n");
    printf("\tContent is %s\n\tAddress is %u\n",
            aStr, aStr);
    printf("\nDetails of second string:\n");
    printf("\tContent is %s\n\tAddress is %u\n",
            bStr, bStr);
```

```
diffAddress = (aStr > bStr
        ? aStr - bStr : bStr - aStr);
printf("\nAddress difference is %u\n\n",
        diffAddress);

printf("First string\n\n");
for (indexStr = 0; indexStr <= SIZE - 1;
        indexStr++)
    printf("%u    %c\n", aStr + indexStr,
            *(aStr + indexStr));
printf("\n\nSecond string\n\n");
for (indexStr - 0; indexStr <- SIZE - 1;
        indexStr++)
    printf("%u    %c\n", bStr + indexStr,
            *(bStr + indexStr));
}

void oopyString(srcStr, destStr)
char *srcStr, destStr[];
    {
    do
        *destStr++ = *srcStr;
    while (*srcStr++ !- '\0');
    }
```

The only difference is in the function copyString() which does not use a local variable, because the neater method of incrementation (by the ++ operator) is utilized.

The printed output is:

STRING 6

First string **987654321**

Details of first string:
    Content is 987654321
    Address is 3732

Details of second string:
    Content is 987654321
    Address is 3722

Address difference is 10

First string

3732   9
3733   8
3734   7
3735   6
3736   5
3737   4
3738   3
3739   2
3740   1
3741

Second string

3722	9
3723	8
3724	7
3725	6
3726	5
3727	4
3728	3
3729	2
3730	1
3731	

It can be seen that there is no difference in form of output. The second version of the copyString() function is to be preferred to the first version in terms of elegance and simplicity.

Chapter 11

Strings and storage

The next stage in the exposition is the copying of a string, where the string is fixed within the program (that is, the string is explicit).

So far we have steered clear of the question of how a string constant is used within a C program. A string constant is a string such as "qwertyuio" which appears in the source program in exactly that form. The constant is "qwertyuio" and is not described by any name.

⬤ Explicit strings and constants

We have steered clear of this question by using gets() to accept strings from the console, we cannot hold off any longer:

```
/* C3P STRING 7 program */

/* Boris Allan */

/*
 * Copying a string by passing a string
 * explicitly as an argument to copyString()
 */

#include <stdio.h>
#define SIZE 10

main()
   {
   void copyString(char *, char *);
   char aStr[SIZE];
   int indexStr = 0;
/*
 * Copy an explicit string "zxcvbnmas"
 * to aStr
 */
   copyString("zxcvbnmas", aStr);
   printf("STRING 7\n\n\nDetails of string:\n");
   printf("\tContent is %s\n\tAddress is %u\n",
         aStr, aStr);
   printf("\nCharacters in string\n\n");
   for (indexStr = 0; indexStr <= SIZE - 1;
         indexStr++)
      printf("%u    %c\n", aStr + indexStr,
            *(aStr + indexStr));
   }
```

```
void copyString(srcStr, destStr)
char *srcStr, destStr[];
    {
    do
        *destStr++ = *srcStr;
    while (*srcStr++ != '\0');
    }
```

The result of executing this program is

STRING 7

Details of string:
  Content is zxcvbnmas
  Address is 3620

Characters in string

3620	*z*
3621	*x*
3622	*c*
3623	*v*
3624	*b*
3625	*n*
3626	*m*
3627	*a*
3628	*s*
3629	

::

PROBLEM 11.1

Construct a function to test whether an address is passed if a string is given explicitly in a function call.

::

● Initializing strings

The final string program uses another C facility, that is, the initialization of a string in a declaration.

```
/* C3P STRING 8 program */

/* Boris Allan */

/*
 * Copying a string, with aStr initialized.
 */

#include <stdio.h>
#define SIZE 10

main()
    {
    void copyString(char *, char *);
    char *aStr = "poiuytrew", bStr[SIZE];
    int diffAddress, indexStr = 0;

    copyString(aStr, bStr);
```

```
    printf("STRING 8\n\nn");
    printf("\nDetails of first string:\n");
    printf("\tContent is %s\n\tAddress is %u\n",
        aStr, aStr);
    printf("\nDetails of second string:\n");
    printf("\tContent is %s\n\tAddress is %u\n",
        bStr, bStr);

    diffAddress = (aStr > bStr
        ? aStr - bStr : bStr - aStr);
    printf("\nAddress difference is %u\n\n",
        diffAddress);

    printf("First string\n\n");
    for (indexStr = 0; indexStr <= SIZE - 1;
        indexStr++)
      printf("%u    %c\n", aStr + indexStr,
            *(aStr + indexStr));
    printf("\n\nSecond string\n\n");
    for (indexStr = 0; indexStr <= SIZE - 1;
        indexStr++)
      printf("%u    %c\n", bStr + indexStr,
            *(bStr + indexStr));
    }


void copyString(srcStr, destStr)
/* Altered argument declarations */
char srcStr[], *destStr;
    {
    do
        *destStr++ = *srcStr;
    while (*srcStr++ != '\0');
    }
```

The action is illustrated by this output:

STRING 8

Details of first string:
    Content is poiuytrew
    Address is 80

Details of second string:
    Content is poiuytrew
    Address is 3730

Address difference is 3650

First string

80   p
81   o
82   i
83   u
84   y
85   t
86   r
87   e
88   w
89

Second string

```
3730  p
3731  o
3732  i
3733  u
3734  y
3735  t
3736  r
3737  e
3738  w
3739
```

If the address of the initialized string is compared with the address of the string passed as an argument (see PROBLEM 11.1), it can be seen that the addresses are the same. Passing a string explicitly as an argument is equivalent to the explicit initialization of a string.

Different C systems will have different methods of dealing with this topic. Systems may vary, so be wary.

::

PROBLEM 11.2

Construct a program to test what happens to addresses when not only is a string initialized in a declaration, but also a string is given explicitly in a function call.

::

▨ Discussion of problems

::

PROBLEM 11.1

Construct a function to test whether an address is passed if a string is given explicitly in a function call.

::

Without more ado:

```
/* C3P PROBLEM 11.1.1 program */

/* Boris Allan */

/*
 * Address of string constant
 * first version
 */

#include <stdio.h>

main()
    {
    int aAddressString(char *);
    aAddressString("zxcvbnmas");
    }

aAddressString(argumentString)
char *argumentString;
    {
    printf("Address is %u/n", argumentString);
    }
```

and the operation of the program should be clear.

The string address is passed as an argument, and the value is printed as an unsigned integer. The result of the program is (for the system on which this program was executed)

Address is 80

which shows that the string constant starts at location 80.

Earlier, we returned a value from a function and it seems a good idea to get the function to return the value of the address. Unless otherwise stipulated, a function is assumed to be capable of returning an integer (int), and if any other type of value is to be returned, then the type has to be given explicitly.

The type of the argument string is declared as a pointer to a character, that is,

```
char *argumentString;
```

and so, if the function is to return the value of argumentString, then the function has to be declared as returning a pointer to a character:

```
char *bAddressString(argumentString)
```

The use of a function to return a value makes a good deal of sense in this case.

The next attempt to construct a function (PROBLEM 11.1.2 program) is not successful on many systems, merely because the function bAddressString() is encountered in the main() function before it is defined.

When the bAddressString() function is encountered in main() the C translator assumes that the function returns an integer (the default). When, later in the program, the bAddressString() function is defined, the type of the function is altered. This normally produces an error.

Program PROBLEM 11.1.2 is thus in error.

```
/* C3P PROBLEM 11.1.2 program */

/* Boris Allan */

/*
 * Address of string constant
 * second version, first attempt
 *
 * Program is in error
 */

#include <stdio.h>

main()
    {
    printf("Address is %u\n",
            bAddressString("zxcvbnmas"));
    }

char *bAddressString(argumentString)
char *argumentString;
    {
    return argumentString;
    }
```

All that is required to make the program execute correctly is to place the definition of bAddressString() before the definition of main(), so that the C translator knows all about bAddressString() before the function is called in main().

```
/* C3P PROBLEM 11.1.3 program */

/* Boris Allan */

/*
 * Address of string constant
 * second version, second attempt
 */

#include <stdio.h>

/*
 * Note that the function does not return
 * an int, but a pointer to char.
 *
 * The function bAddressString() has to be
 * declared prior to main(), otherwise C
 * will assume the function returns an int.
 *
 * If the function is defined after main()
 * then there will be a 'redefinition' error,
 * that is, the int function will be  char * .
 */

char *bAddressString(argumentString)
char *argumentString;
    {
    return argumentString;
    }

main()
    {
    printf("Address is %u\n",
        bAddressString("zxcvbnmas"));
    }
```

The result of this program is also

Address is 80

that is, for the system in use, the constant is stored at the same location.

It is rather inconvenient to have to remember the order in which functions have to be defined, and at times it is almost impossible to work out a sensible ordering.

Worrying about the order does not matter if the value returned from a function is the default (that is, integer) or there is no value returned. In the case where the value differs from the default, however, the C translator has to know what is expected from the function.

If (as will happen in complex systems) there is more than one compiled segment to be linked, then each separate segment will need to know if there are unusual types returned by a function. The problem is resolved by declaring the type of a function before it is used: sometimes known as a forward declaration.

We have already followed this practice (especially with void functions). A forward declaration is illustrated in PROBLEM 11.1.4:

```
/* C3P PROBLEM 11.1.4 program */

/* Boris Allan */

/*
 * Address of string constant
 * second version, third attempt
 * first style of declaration
 */

#include <stdio.h>

/*
 * Forward declaration, with complete
 * information about data types
 */
char *bAddressString(char *);
```

```
main()
    {
    printf("Address is %u\n",
           bAddressString("zxcvbnmas"));
    }


char *bAddressString(argumentString)
char *argumentString;
    {
    return argumentString;
    }
```

This form of forward declaration, that is,

```
char *bAddressString(char *);
```

not only specifies the type of the value returned by the function as
char *bAddressString() but also specifies the type of the
argument as (char *).

In the case of some C language systems — including most older
UNIX C compilers — the specification of the type of the argument is
not possible, and the forward function declaration has to take the
form given in PROBLEM 11.1.4.1:

```
/* C3P PROBLEM 11.1.4.1 program */

/* Boris Allan */

/*
 * Address of string constant
 * second version, third attempt,
 * second style of declaration
 */

#include <stdio.h>

/*
 * Forward declaration, with no
 * information about the data types
 * for the function argument(s)
 */
char *bAddressString();

main()
    {
    printf("Address is %u\n",
          bAddressString("zxcvbnmas"));
    }

char *bAddressString(argumentString)
char *argumentString;
    {
    return argumentString;
    }
```

The restricted version of the forward declaration is admissible on all C language systems but, as there are no checks on the argument data types, the security is less.

If the argument types are specified in a forward definition, then when the function is called later (and — as in this case — defined) there are checks for compatibility. A fully specified forward declaration is an extra check on the correctness of your program.

C3P will use the full form of declaration, that is, with complete specification of argument types.

:::

PROBLEM 11.2

Construct a program to test what happens to addresses when not only is a string initialized in a declaration, but also a string is given explicitly in a function call.

:::

To solve this problem we had best make use of the bAddressString() function, and here is one solution:

```
/* C3P PROBLEM 11.2 program */

/* Boris Allan */

/*
 * Addresses of initialized string
 * and string passed explicitly as
 * an argument to a function
 */
```

```
#include <stdio.'h>

char *bAddressString(char *);

main()
    {
    char *initString = "asdfghjkl";
    printf("Initialized address is %u\n",
            bAddressString(initString));
    printf("Argument address is %u\n",
            bAddressString("zxcvbnmas"));
    }


    char *bAddressString(argumentString)
    char *argumentString;
        {
        return argumentString;
        }
```

which has the output

Initialized address is 80
Argument address is 117

Thus it can be seen that when there are two explicit strings, memory is set aside for the two strings at different locations (it would be impossible to share the same locations).

   The initialized string extends from 80 to 89 (10 locations including \0), and there seems to be a gap from 90 to 116 (that is, 27 locations). This gap is filled by the string "Argument address is %u\n" plus extras such as \0. Even string constants in printf() have to be stored somewhere in memory ...

Part Four

Data types

In this part we will discuss the characteristics of data types in C, and the relationships between the types.

As C is such an open language, it is possible to use C to find out more about the nature of data than most conventional languages.

Chapter 12

Bit patterns

As a language, C is not noted for a particular suitability for floating point arithmetic, though versions differ in the quality of implementation of floating point arithmetic.

C is most at home in the treatment of integer quantities, or data types (such as characters and, therefore, strings) which are expressed in the form of integers (a character has an ASCII value).

An integer is a number which cannot have a fractional part. A floating point variable might have an integral value (say, 5) but, when the floating point value of 5 is divided by 2, the floating point variable can store the value 2.5. An integer variable can store 5, or 2, or 3, but the value 2.5 cannot be stored.

The basic data type for integers in C is that declared as int, and normally an int occupies two bytes of storage (a char occupies one byte as a general rule). There are 8 bits to a byte for most computers, and so a two byte int is equivalent to a binary number of up to 16 bits.

An int in C is stored as a sixteen bit number for the majority of older systems — with newer 32 bit machines, an int is often four bytes. There are different lengths of integers (short and long, for example) but we will concentrate on the standard length integer.

Before examining floating point numbers I will study various characteristics of the basic integer types, because integers are crucial to understanding the operation of C. We will concentrate on the manipulation of signed and unsigned integers, and start with a 4 bit integer to illustrate two's complement arithmetic.

PROBLEM 12.1

Write a function to convert a positive denary integer into an 8 bit
binary integer, where the result is stored as an 8 character string.

● Two's complement arithmetic

Study this table of binary values, and look at the two denary
interpretations of the binary values. Each binary value is a 4 bit
number.

BINARY VALUE	UNSIGNED DENARY	SIGNED DENARY
0000	0	0
0001	1	1
0010	2	2
0011	3	3
0100	4	4
0101	5	5
0110	6	6
0111	7	7
1000	8	−8
1001	9	−7
1010	10	−6
1011	11	−5
1100	12	−4
1101	13	−3
1110	14	−2
1111	15	−1
0000	0	0

The column which is headed UNSIGNED DENARY is what we normally take as the value of a binary number. If, however, we have to change from a denary number to a binary number, the translation is not so certain.

For example: *what is the binary equivalent of the denary number –2?*

On the one hand, we can say that the binary equivalent of denary –2 is –10 but, unfortunately, on computers we can store only positive binary values. There is no provision for the sign of a binary value built into most computers as part of the hardware (there are a few exceptions). It is possible to use a version of –10 as the binary equivalent of –2, but to implement this equivalence requires a far more complex translator.

On the other hand (for a 4 bit binary number), we can note that –2 + 2 = 0, and that 1110 + 0010 = 0000 (the number wraps round). It seems, therefore, that the binary equivalent of (denary) –2 is possibly 1110. If we perform the (denary) addition –2 + 3 = 1, the binary equivalent is thus 1110 + 0011 = 0001 — so consistency is maintained.

Consistency is not maintained, however, in 7 + 1 = 8 because (in binary) 0111 + 0001 = 1000, which means that 7 + 1 = –8 according to the above convention for signed numbers. The range of possible operations on numbers is, therefore, subject to restrictions in many programming languages.

The system used above for negative numbers is known as *two's complement*, and is that shown in the column headed SIGNED DENARY. Note that negative numbers are distinguished by a leading (leftmost, most significant) 1 bit, thus the most significant bit can be regarded as a *sign* bit.

● Signed integers

First of all, a problem.

∷∷∷

PROBLEM 12.2

Write a function to convert a negative denary integer into an 8 bit
binary integer, where the result is stored as an 8 character string.

∷∷∷

The information you have imbued in the analysis of the above
problem may help you to understand the strange happenings of this
section.
   Here is a program which performs simple operations on integers

```
/* C3P INTEGER 1 program */

/* Boris Allan */

/*
 * Use of signed integer and
 * effects of doubling.
 */

#include <stdio.h>

/* Setting constants */
#define START 1
#define NUMBER 20
#define MULTIPLIER 2
```

```
main()
    {
/*
 * Declarations and initializations
 */
    int multValue = START, loopCount = NUMBER;

    printf("\nINTEGER 1\n");

/*
 * The character pair %% are printed
 * as the single character '%'
 */
    printf("\tint value, %%d, 2\n\n");

    while (0 < loopCount--)
        {
        multValue = multValue * MULTIPLIER;
        printf("%d\n", multValue);
        };
    }
```

We will not discuss this program at length, but merely give the output of an activation of the program [1]:

INTEGER 1
  int value, %d, 2

2
4
8
16
32
64

```
128
256
512
1024
2048
4096
8192
16384
-32768
0
0
0
0
0
```

This program takes the START value 1, a MULTIPLIER of 2, and iterates through a while–loop for a NUMBER of times (20). At each iteration the multValue is multiplied by the MULTIPLIER, and the result of the multiplication output is a signed denary integer (that is, %d).

As can be seen, the final outcome is to make the multValue equal to zero. You can explain this by reference to the discussion of PROBLEM 12.1.

Remember that, as a 16 bit binary number, denary 32768 is the same as denary −32768 is the same as binary 10000000 00000000, and twice binary 10000000 00000000 is 00000000 00000000 (which is denary 0). The next program modifies the above outline.

```
/* C3P INTEGER 2 program */


/* Boris Allan */


/*
 * Use of signed integer and
 * effects of trebling.
 */
```

```
#include <stdio.h>

#define START 1
#define NUMBER 20
#define MULTIPLIER 3

main()
   {
   int multValue - START,
      loopCount = NUMBER;

   printf("\nINTEGER 2\n");
   printf("\tint value, %%d, 3\n\n");
   while (0 < loopCount--)
      {
      multValue *= MULTIPLIER;
      printf("%d\n", multValue);
      };
   }
```

to produce a new output, for the case where the MULTIPLIER is equal
to 3.

INTEGER 2
  int value, %d, 3

3
9
27
81
243
729
2187

6561
19683
−6487
−19461
7153
21459
−1159
−3477
−10431
−31293
−28343
−19493
7057

If we were not prepared for such an eventuality, then we might be very surprised to find that 19683 * 3 = −6487, but we can easily see how such an event takes place.

Expressed in binary, the denary number 19683 is equivalent to 01001100 11100011, which when muliplied by (denary) 3 gives 11100110 10101001 in binary, or −6487 as a complement value.

The key characteristic of both programs is that the multValue is defined as a signed integer (the declaration int multValue means that multValue is to be treated as signed integer). A signed integer is able to take positive or negative values, but an integer defined as being unsigned is constrained to positive values alone.

● Unsigned integers

Try the equivalent programs with unsigned integers.

```
/* C3P INTEGER 3 program */

/* Boris Allan */

/*
 * Use of unsigned integer, and doubling
 */
```

```
#include <stdio.h>

#define START 1
#define NUMBER 20
#define MULTIPLIER 2

main()
    {
    unsigned multValue = START;
    int loopCount = NUMBER;

    printf("\nINTEGER 3\n");
    printf("\tunsigned value, %%u, 2\n\n");

    while (0 < loopCount--)
        printf("%u\n", multValue *= MULTIPLIER);
    }
```

This program changes the type of multValue to unsigned, but then merely repeats the program INTEGER 1 in all other aspects, apart from the printing of the value. The two lines to be compared are

```
printf("%d\n", multValue);
printf("%u\n", multValue);
```

so that in the first line the printf() function is informed that multValue is a signed decimal (denary) integer, by use of the %d format control, whereas in the second line the value is defined as being an unsigned decimal integer, by use of the %u control.

The new outcome is·

INTEGER 3
  unsigned value, %u, 2

2
4
8
16
32
64
128
256
512
1024
2048
4096
8192
16384
32768
0
0
0
0
0

The comparisons with the results of INTEGER 1 are illuminating, but first another program (INTEGER 4)

```
/* C3P INTEGER 4 program */

/* Boris Allan */

/*
 * Use of unsigned integer and
 * effects of trebling.
 */
```

```
#include <stdio.h>

#define START 1
#define NUMBER 20
#define MULTIPLIER 3

main()
    {
    unsigned multValue = START;
    int loopCount = NUMBER;

    printf("\nINTEGER 4\n");
    printf("\tunsigned value, %%u, 3\n\n");

    while (0 < loopCount--)
        printf("%u\n", multValue *= MULTIPLIER);
    }
```

which prints out the following information:

INTEGER 4
  unsigned value, %u, 3

3
9
27
81
243
729
2187
6561
19683
59049
46075
7153

21459

64377

62059

55105

34243

37193

46043

7057

The output for INTEGER 4 helps explain the output for INTEGER 2.

The value of 19683 * 3 is 59049 as an unsigned (positive) integer in INTEGER 4, which is equivalent to the complemented (negative) value −(65536 − 59049) = −6847 in INTEGER 2.

The value of 59049 * 3 = 177147 which is equivalent to 46075 (modulo 65536, because the unsigned integer occupies two bytes). The unsigned 46075 is equivalent to −19461 as a signed integer.

■ Discussion of problems

PROBLEM 12.1

Write a function to convert a positive denary integer into an 8 bit binary integer, where the result is stored as an 8 character string.

The first point to establish is how it is possible to convert a denary number into a binary number. Consider the denary number 25, which has a binary equivalent of 0011001 (as an 8 bit number).

If the denary number is odd, then the rightmost bit of the binary number must be a 1: if the number is even, then the rightmost bit is 0.

The rightmost bit of the binary number corresponding to 25 (which is odd) must, therefore, be a 1. If we subtract the value of the rightmost bit (in this case, 1) the result is 24: taking 24 and dividing by 2 gives the result 12.

If we treat the denary value 12 as the number to convert to binary, then the rightmost bit is o (because 12 is even), thus the second bit of the binary number (corresponding to denary 25) is o. 12 less 0 (its rightmost bit) is 12, and half 12 is 6. The rightmost bit (for the denary value 6) is thus o, and the third bit (corresponding to denary 25) is 0. Half of 6 is 3, so the rightmost bit (corresponding to 3) is 1 and the fourth bit (corresponding to 25) is 1.

3 less 1 is 2, and half 2 is 1, so the remaining bit is equal to 1, and thus the fifth bit (corresponding to denary 25) is 1. Filling up the remaining bits with 0 produces the binary number 00011001.

Here is the sequence:

NUMBER	BIT
25	1
12	0
6	0
3	1
1	1
0	0

We implement the above sequence of operations (the algorithm) in the following program.

```
/* C3P PROBLEM 12.1.1 program */

/* Boris Allan */

/*
 * Convert a denary integer
 * to an 8 bit binary number.
 */

#include <stdio.h>
/* Number of bits in number */
#define BITS 8
```

```
/* Is the number odd? */
oddNo(inputValue)
int inputValue;
    {
    (1 & inputValue);
    }


/*
 * Return a ´1´ or ´0´ character
 * depending on whether argument is
 * the number 1 or 0. Exit if the
 * number is not 1 or 0.
 */
char binChar(inputValue)
int inputValue;
    {
    if (inputValue == 1)
        return(´1´);
    else
        if (inputValue == 0)
            return(´0´);
        else /* error message */
            {
            fprintf(stderr, "binChar error");
            exit (1);
            }
    }
```

```
/*
 * Conversion function. First argument
 * is input value, and second argument
 * is a pointer to the start of a string.
 */
void decToBin(inVal,outStr)
int inVal;
char *outStr;
    {
    int tempBit, indexStr = BITS - 1,
          oddNo(int);
    char tempChar, binChar(int);


/* End the string */
    outStr[BITS] = '\0';


/*
 * Generate bits from rightmost bit of
 * binary number (stored in outStr).
 */
    while (indexStr >= 0)
       {
       tempBit = oddNo(inVal);
       tempChar = binChar(tempBit);
       outStr[indexStr--] = tempChar;
       inVal = (inVal - tempBit)/2;
       };
    }
```

```
main()
  {
  char binNum[BITS+1], binChar(int);
  int decNum, oddNo(int);
  void decToBin(int, char *);
/*
 * Note that the scanf() function is given the
 * ADDRESS of the variable decNum, by use of &.
 * &decNum gives the address of decNum.
 * The address is used because C functions call by
 * copy, and not by name.
 */
  while (printf("Denary is "), fflush(stdout),
         scanf("%d",&decNum), decNum != 0)
    {
    decToBin(decNum, binNum);
    printf("Binary is %s\n\n", binNum);
    };
  }
```

The main() function declares a string (binNum) of BITS bits (BITS
is defined earlier in the source code), and a signed integer known as
decNum.

The while–loop operates by asking for a denary number, inputs that
number (by use of scanf() after flushing the output buffer), and
then checks to see if the number is equal to zero. All four actions are
activated at each pass through the loop, because the actions are
separated by commas.

In the body of the loop, there is a call to the decToBin()
function, a function which takes two arguments: the denary number,
and the string pointer which is to store the binary number. After the
conversion the binary number is output as the string binNum. The
body of the while–loop in main() ends at this action, and the three
initial actions are activated.

The program inputs denary numbers until a value of 0 is entered at
the console (that is, on stdin).

If we track backwards through the source code, we encounter the function decToBin() with two arguments — the first argument is an integer (inVal), and the second is a pointer to a character string (outStr).

Two local/automatic integers are declared, and one is initialized to the value BITS − 1 (indexStr) whereas the other is merely declared without initialization (tempBit). The integer indexStr is used to index characters within the binary number stored as the string to which outStr points. The other local variable is the character tempChar.

A string is terminated by the character \0, and so the first action of the function is to terminate the string outStr by a \0 at a location which is BITS+1 characters on from the start (that is, *(outStr + BITS) or outStr[BITS]).

Once the string is ended with a \0 we can fill in the characters of the string without worrying about termination.

In the while–loop, we continue while the value of indexStr is greater than or equal to zero (that is, we are within the confines of the string). The input integer (inVal) is checked to see if it is odd or even, and the value 1 or 0 returned to be stored in the local integer tempBit.

Depending on the value of the tempBit, the function binChar() either returns a character '1' or '0' (or exits the program with an error, if the argument is neither 1 nor 0).

We have to distinguish between the integer 1 and the character '1' when we store the value, because the ASCII value corresponding to the character '1' is 49. The tempChar is then assigned to the appropriate location of the string, and the indexStr decremented by one unit. There is no real use for tempChar, and the variable has been used merely to clarify structure.

The value of inVal is modified by subtracting the value of the tempBit, and dividing by 2. This line could also be written

```
inVal -= tempBit;
inVal /= 2;
```

with an improvement in efficiency for some translators.

The oddNo() function is very simple, in that it takes an integer argument (inputValue), and in the body of the function there is an example of the bitwise operation & (the bitwise AND)

```
(1 & inputValue)
```

which produces the value 1 if the number is odd, and produces 0 if the number is even. It might be argued that to use a bitwise operation begs the question (as we are constructing a binary number), and so an equivalent operation is

```
(inputValue != (inputValue/2)*2)
```

Note that to alter the oddNo() function in this manner has no effect on any other part of the program. As far as other functions are concerned, the input is the same, and so is the output. The function has no side effects, that is, nothing out with the oddNo() function is affected by the operation of the function [2].

The line

```
(1 & inputValue);
```

is not an assignment, in that nothing is performed with the result of the bitwise comparison. The value is left as the result of the operation of the function: it is the result of the function which is assigned to the variable in decToBin().

The line can be modified to produce an identical result

```
return (1 & inputValue);
```

but to use the return command means that the function is automatically ended at that point. In the case of oddNo() the function does end with this line, but in other functions there can be more than one possible return from a function — which brings us to binChar().

Another way a function can be ended is with an exit command, as illustrated in the function binChar(), but an exit means that the complete program is terminated. An exit is often used, as in the case of binChar(), to abort a program in the case of some error.

It is possible to give an *errorLevel* (in the case of binChar() the errorLevel is 1). If the program is executed from within another program, then the errorLevel can indicate the type of error for recovery routines.

In binChar(), the function is declared as returning a character (normally it is assumed that a function returns an integer). The argument (inputValue) is an integer and if the integer is equal to 1 then the character ´1´ is returned, else a check is made to see if the value is 0 (and ´0´ is returned). If neither of the above is true an error message is output on the standard error stream (stderr) and an exit is made with errorLevel 1 (successful execution produces an automatic errorLevel of 0).

Execution of the above program produces the following output:

Denary is **1**
Binary is 00000001

Denary is **12**
Binary is 00001100

Denary is **123**
Binary is 01111011

Denary is **1234**
Binary is 11010010

Denary is **12345**
Binary is 00111001

Denary is **126**
Binary is 01111110

Denary is **127**
Binary is 01111111

Denary is **128**
Binary is 10000000

Denary is **254**
Binary is 11111110

Denary is **255**
Binary is 11111111

Denary is **256**
Binary is 00000000

Denary is **0**

The largest positive denary integer which can be stored as a signed integer in two bytes is 32767, but the largest unsigned number which can be stored in an 8 bit byte is 255.

Any denary number greater than 255, therefore, is stored as a binary number modulo 256. The value of 256 modulo 256 is 0, and thus the 8 bit binary version of denary 256 is 00000000.

If the binary number is to be stored in 16 bits, we have to use a long integer which is defined as being no smaller than an integer, but which may be longer (on the system being used, a long integer occupies 32 bits).

Here is a modified version of the above program, plus some specimen output, to accommodate 16 bit binary numbers. The program is almost the same as PROBLEM 12.1.1, except for the number of BITS, and the use of the %ld format control (long integer).

```
/* C3P PROBLEM 12.1.2 program */

/* Boris Allan */

/*
 * Convert a long denary integer
 * to a 16 bit binary number.
 */
```

```
#include <stdio.h>
#define BITS 16

oddNo(inputValue)
long inputValue; /* change */
    {
    (int) (1 & inputValue);
    }


char binChar(inputValue)
int inputValue;
    {
    if (inputValue == 1)
       return('1');
    else
       if (inputValue == 0)
          return('0');
       else
          {
          fprintf(stderr, "binChar error");
          exit (1);
          }
    }


void decToBin(inVal,outStr)
long inVal; /* change */
char *outStr;
    {
    int tempBit, indexStr = BITS - 1,
          oddNo(int);
    char tempChar, binChar(int);

    outStr[BITS] = '\0';
```

```
        while (indexStr >= 0)
         , {
            tempBit = oddNo(inVal);
            tempChar = binChar(tempBit);
            outStr[indexStr--] = tempChar;
            inVal = (inVal - tempBit)/2;
            };
        }


    main()
        {
        char binNum[BITS], binChar(int);
        long decNum;
        void decToBin(long, char *),
        int oddNo(long); /* changes */
        while (printf("Denary is "), fflush(stdout),
               scanf("%ld",&decNum), decNum != 0)
            {
            decToBin(decNum, binNum);
            printf("Binary is %s\n\n", binNum);
            };
        }
```

The output is of the form

Denary is **1**
Binary is 0000000000000001

Denary is **12**
Binary is 0000000000001100

Denary is **123**
Binary is 0000000001111011

Denary is **1234**
Binary is 0000010011010010

Denary is **12345**
Binary is 0011000000111001

Denary is **123456**
Binary is 1110001001000000

Denary is **1234567**
Binary is 1101011010000111

Denary Is **126**
Binary is 0000000001111110

Denary is **127**
Binary is 0000000001111111

Denary is **128**
Binary is 0000000010000000

Denary is **254**
Binary is 0000000011111110

Denary is **255**
Binary is 0000000011111111

Denary is **256**
Binary is 0000000100000000

Denary is **32766**
Binary is 0111111111111110

Denary is **32767**
Binary is 0111111111111111

Denary is **32768**
Binary is 1000000000000000

Denary is **65534**
Binary is 111111111111110

Denary is **65535**
Binary is 111111111111111

Denary is **65536**
Binary is 0000000000000000

Denary is **0**

It is well worth comparing the two programs, and an examination of the output of the second program reveals a good deal about the results of the first program.

●●●

PROBLEM 12.2

Write a function to convert a negative denary integer into an 8 bit binary integer, where the result is stored as an 8 character string.

●●●

Before we construct such a program, first we will examine a new form of control construct. After the examination, we will produce a program to convert negative denary numbers.

In the binChar() function in the programs for the preceding problem, there is a multiple comparison by use of the if ... else control construct, and the PROBLEM 12.2.1 program uses a different control construct.

```
/* C3P PROBLEM 12.2.1 program */

/* Boris Allan */

/*
 * Use of switch control statement
 */

#include <stdio.h>
#define BITS 8

       .

       .

       .
/*
 * New use of the switch
 * control statement.
 */
char binChar(inputValue)
int inputValue;
    {
/*
 * 'break' is not necessary in this case,
 * because each 'case' ends with a 'return' or
 * 'exit', but the use of break is advisable.
 */
    switch (inputValue)
       {
       case 1 :
          return('1'); break;
       case 0 :
          return('0'); break;
       default :
          fprintf(stderr, "binChar error");
          exit(1); break;
       }
    }
```

```
        .

        .

        .

    main()
        {
        .

        .

        .

        }
```

The main difference in this particular program arises with the use of
switch in binChar().

In the first version of this program, we used nested if constructs
to decide between three choices, and in this second version of 8 bit
binary conversion we state the three choices by use of case.

The three alternatives are:

1️⃣   case 1 :
            return('1'); break;

That is, return the ASCII value corresponding to the
character '1'.

2️⃣   case 0 :
            return('0'); break;

That is, return the ASCII value corresponding to the
character '0'.

3️⃣   default :
            fprintf(stderr, "binChar error");
            exit(1); break;

That is, file print (fprintf()) *binChar error* on the standard
error stream (stderr) and exit with an errorLevel of 1.

The break command means that the switch construct is terminated,
otherwise it is possible for the program control to continue through the
remaining cases. break can also be used to leave a loop construct —
a sign of bad programming.

The output from this program is exactly equivalent to that from the
first program:

Denary is **-1**
Binary is 11111111

Denary is **-12**
Binary is 11110100

Denary is **-123**
Binary is 10000101

Denary is **-1234**
Binary is 00101110

Denary is **-12345**
Binary is 11000111

Denary is **-126**
Binary is 10000010

Denary is **-127**
Binary is 10000001

Denary is **-128**
Binary is 10000000

Denary is **-254**
Binary is 00000010

Denary is **-255**
Binary is 00000001

Denary is **-256**
Binary is 00000000

Denary is **0**

This is exactly the same as the output from the first program for the same input values.

The main point to notice for this set of input values is that the input values are all negative. We have, in fact, constructed a conversion program for positive denary numbers which, we have discovered, works with negative binary numbers.

This ability to cope with signed input is another reason why two's complement arithmetic is used for integers: the action of conversion is identical for positive and negative numbers. The solution to the first two problems is thus the same program.

Finally, here is the output for the 16 bit conversion program – for specimen negative numbers:

Denary is –1
Binary is 111111111111111

Denary is –12
Binary is 111111111110100

Denary is –123
Binary is 111111110000101

Denary is –1234
Binary is 111110110010110

Denary is –12345
Binary is 110011111000111

Denary is –123456
Binary is 0001110111000000

Denary is –1234567
Binary is 0010100101111001

Denary is –126
Binary is 111111110000010

Denary is –127
Binary is 111111110000001

Denary is **-128**
Binary is 1111111110000000

Denary is **-254**
Binary is 1111111100000010

Denary is **-255**
Binary Is 1111111100000001

Denary is **-256**
Binary is 1111111100000000

Denary is **-32766**
Binary is 1000000000000010

Denary is **-32767**
Binary is 1000000000000001

Denary is **-32768**
Binary is 1000000000000000

Denary is **-65534**
Binary is 0000000000000010

Denary is **-65535**
Binary is 0000000000000001

Denary is **-65536**
Binary Is 0000000000000000

Denary is **0**

Notes

[1]   On a few C systems the INTEGER programs will not execute in the manner described, because there will be overflow errors. In this case it is still possible to follow the development of the argument from an examination of the output, as given with each program.

[2]   It is good programming practice to try to construct functions with as few side effects as possible, because programs are less unstable, that is, less susceptible to strange happenings within functions. Try to make your functions as independent as possible: for example, try not to depend upon changing the values of global variables.

Chapter 13

Integers

In this chapter we continue the investigation of types of integer, and
the ways in which such types relate to each other.

We will start by looking at the relationship between signed and
unsigned integers, moving to a specification of the rules for conversion
between integral quantities.

● The value as a bit pattern

C distinguishes between the variable, multValue, and the way in
which the variable is treated: consider this program

```
/* C3P INTEGER 5 program */

/* Boris Allan */

/*
 * Signed integer, trebling, and
 * %u format in printf().
 */

#include <stdio.h>
#define START 1
#define NUMBER 20
#define MULTIPLIER 3
```

```
main()
    {
    int multValue = START, loopCount = NUMBER;
    printf("\nINTEGER 5\n");
    printf("\tint value, %%u, 3\n\n");
    while (0 < loopCount--)
        printf("%u\n",
               multValue *= MULTIPLIER);
    }
```

where there is a signed integer multValue, but the printf()
function is given an unsigned format control (%u), and note we have
lost one excess line by using

```
    printf("%u\n", multValue *= MULTIPLIER);
```

in that the assignment and the print value are given as one.

The changed printf() does not affect the performance of the
program, but the outcome is interesting:

INTEGER 5
  int value, %u, 3

3
9
27
81
243
729
2187
6561
19683
59049
46075
7153
21459
64377

62059
55105
34243
37193
46043
7057

The printed output of INTEGER 5 is exactly the same as that of INTEGER 4, so it seems as if the format control is more important than the declaration.

The variable multValue is declared as being signed, but the printed text appears exactly the same as if multVal was declared as an unsigned integer. Furthermore, if the program INTEGER 6 is studied

```
/* C3P INTEGER 6 program */

/* Boris Allan */

/*
 * Unsigned integer, trebling, and
 * %d format in printf().
 */

#include <stdio.h>
#define FST 1
#define NO 20
#define TIMES 3

main()
    {
    unsigned multVal = FST; int loopCt = NO;
    printf("\nINTEGER 6\n");
    printf("\tunsigned value, %%d, 3\n\n");
    while (0 < loopCt--)
        printf("%d\n", multVal *= TIMES);
    }
```

In this program the order is reversed, in that the variable multVal is declared as unsigned but the print format control is signed (%d). The result of the program is this listing of values:

INTEGER 6
  unsigned value, %d, 3

3
9
27
81
243
729
2187
6561
19683
–6487
–19461
7153
21459
–1159
–3477
–10431
–31293
–28343
–19493
7057

The above output for INTEGER 6 again shows the preeminence of the format control.

::

PROBLEM 13.1

Write a program to illustrate all the options given in the INTEGER
programs, in the one program.

::

We have reached the point at which you may think that it does not
matter whether a variable is declared an int or an unsigned. The
declaration does matter, and the next section shows why.

● Comparing integers

Here is a simple program which defines two constants LOW and HIGH
(of value 2000 and 40000), and then assigns those values to both
signed and unsigned integers.
   The signed values (lowInt and highInt) are compared for size,
as are the unsigned values (lowUnsgnd and highUnsgnd). The
results of the comparison are then output on stdout.

```
/* C3P COMPARE INTEGERS program */

/* Boris Allan */

/*
 * Use of comparison operators
 * and effects of integer type.
 */

#include <stdio.h>
#define LOW 2000
#define HIGH 40000
```

```
main()
    {
    int lowInt = LOW, highInt = HIGH;
    unsigned lowUnsgnd = LOW,
            highUnsgnd = HIGH;
    printf("COMPARE INTEGERS\n\n");
    printf("Signed ints %d %d\n", LOW, HIGH);
    if (lowInt < highInt)
        printf("lowInt < highInt\n\n");
    else
        printf("lowInt >= highInt\n\n");
    printf("Unsgnd ints %u %u\n", LOW, HIGH);
    if (lowUnsgnd < highUnsgnd)
        printf("lowUnsgnd < highUnsgnd\n\n");
    else
        printf("lowUnsgnd >= highUnsgnd\n\n");
    }
```

and the result of executing this program:

COMPARE INTEGERS

Signed ints 2000 –25536
lowInt >= highInt

Unsgnd ints 2000 40000
lowUnsgnd < highUnsgnd

When the value of 40000 is assigned to a signed integer (that is, highInt), the result is that C considers the value to be –25536 (because of complement arithmetic). If the two signed values are compared, therefore, the lowInt (2000 assigned) is not less than highInt (40000 assigned), because 2000 is greater than –25536 [1].

It can be seen, therefore, that the declaration is important: the declaration defines the nature of the action of C with respect to operators such as > or /.

The %d and %u format controls for the printf() function act differently from the operators, in that the number in question is treated as a pattern of bits, and is not interpreted further.

That is, the printf() function does not recognize the distinction between (for example) signed and unsigned integers declared as such, because the function knows only how to output a pattern of bits in the form of a signed or an unsigned integer.

We have used the cast facility previously, and the next program makes use of the cast to investigate comparisons.

```
/* C3P CASTING INTEGERS program */

/* Boris Allan */

/*
 * Use of comparison operators and effects
 * of casting integer types.
 */

#include <stdio.h>
#define LOW 2000
#define HIGH 40000

main()
    {
    int lowInt = LOW, highInt = HIGH;
    unsigned lowUnsgnd = LOW,
            highUnsgnd = HIGH;
    printf("CASTING INTEGERS\n\n");

    printf("(unsigned) ints %d %d\n", LOW, HIGH);
    if ((unsigned)lowInt < (unsigned) highInt)
        printf("lowInt < highInt\n\n");
    else
        printf("lowInt >= highInt\n\n");
```

```
    printf("(int) unsigned %u %u\n", LOW, HIGH);
    if ((int) lowUnsgnd < (int) highUnsgnd)
        printf("lowUnsgnd < highUnsgnd\n\n");
    else
        printf("lowUnsgnd >= highUnsgnd\n\n");

    if (highUnsgnd == highInt)
        printf("highUnsgnd == highInt\n\n");
    else
        printf("highUnsgnd != highInt\n\n");

    if (lowUnsgnd < highInt)
        printf("lowUnsgnd < highInt\n\n");
    else
        printf("lowUnsgnd >= highInt\n\n");

    if (highInt > lowUnsgnd)
        printf("highInt > lowUnsgnd\n\n");
    else
        printf("highInt <= lowUnsgnd\n\n");
}
```

The results are interesting in that the effect of casting is to change the way in which the C translator interprets the comparison. A further notable characteristic is the fact that, in the final three comparisons where the types differ either side of the comparison, C treats both values as if they were unsigned types.

We will examine this conversion of types after showing the result of CASTING INTEGERS:

CASTING INTEGERS

(unsigned) ints 2000 −25536
lowInt < highInt

(int) unsigned 2000 40000
lowUnsgnd >= highUnsgnd

highUnsgnd == highInt

lowUnsgnd < highInt

highInt > lowUnsgnd

● The types of integers

In the next chapter we will study floating point numbers, but first a taxonomy of types of integer (including characters).

There are four sizes of bit pattern which can produce an integral result (the four basic types of integral value):

char
: A bit pattern which represents an ASCII character [2], thus a character is of at least 7 bits (and normally 8 bits, or the conventional byte). As far as C is concerned, a char is an 8 bit integer.

short int
: Frequently is written as short. A short integer is a bit pattern with (normally) at least 16 bits (two bytes [3]), and no more bits than an ordinary integer.

int
: A bit pattern considered to represent an integer, and is normally at least 16 bits — the next most common size is 32 bits.

long int
: Frequently is written as long. A long integer is a bit pattern with at least as many bits as the ordinary integer, and is often twice as long as an ordinary integer.

The basic notion which underpins the sizes of the various types of integer for any system is that in some way the simple int should provide the optimum size for a particular machine. All that is certain is that the sizes are in this order:

```
char <= short <= int <= long
```

Apart from char, all the above types are signed, in that the bit pattern is assumed to be interpreted as a two's complement value. The char may be considered to be intrinsically signed or unsigned, depending on the system in use.

All the above types can be treated as unsigned, in that the bit pattern is assumed to be a positive binary number. A type is declared as unsigned by prefixing the signed type by the designation unsigned, for example:

```
unsigned char
unsigned short int
unsigned short
unsigned int
unsigned
unsigned long int
unsigned long
```

though if the char is already unsigned, then the first line is unnecessary.

In general, if the types of operands differ in any arithmetic operation then the usual arithmetic conversions in C are according to the following sequence (where the types float and double will be examined in the next chapter).

Before any other conversions take place in many systems certain changes are made to existing types, with the result that only ints, longs, and doubles are left (chars, shorts, and floats are converted):

    1 Any operands of type char or short are converted to int,

    2 any operands of type unsigned char or unsigned short are converted to unsigned int, and

    3 any operands of type float are converted to double.

    4 IF the type of either operand is double, the other operand is converted to double, and that is the type of the result of the operation, ELSE

    5 IF the type of either operand is unsigned long, the other operand is converted to unsigned long, and that is the type of the result of the operation, ELSE

6 IF the type of either operand is long, the other operand is converted to long, and that is the type of the result of the operation, ELSE

7 IF either operand is unsigned int, the other operand is converted to unsigned int, and that is the type of the result of the operation, ELSE

8 Both operands are int, and that is the type of the result of the operation.

Your own system might have a slightly different way of organizing precedence — it will pay to check your system's documentation. In the comparison

```
if (lowUnsgnd < highInt)
     printf("lowUnsgnd < highInt\n\n");
else
     printf("lowUnsgnd >= highInt\n\n");
```

(from the program CASTING INTEGERS) lowUnsgnd is 2000 and highInt is –25536, so that it would appear that lowUnsgnd is greater than highInt. The two operands (lowUnsgnd, highInt) are of different types, and so — going through the above sequence — we have to use

7 IF either operand is unsigned int, the other operand is converted to unsigned int, and that is the type of the result of the operation.

which is why the comparisons in CASTING INTEGERS produce the correct results.

Integer conversions

At times the system has to convert from one integral type to another, and the following list gives one system's rules for conversion from the signed and unsigned types. Microsoft C running under MSDOS or XENIX — a version of C which has signed characters with short being equivalent to int):

char TO short   Preserve the signed value.

char TO long   Preserve the signed value.

char TO unsigned char
>   Preserve the bit pattern, for example, −1 becomes 255.

char TO unsigned short
>   Change to a signed short, and convert short to unsigned short.

char TO unsigned long
>   Change to a signed long, and convert long to unsigned long.

short TO char   Preserve the low-order (rightmost, least significant) byte.

short TO int   Identical size.

short TO long   Preserve the signed value.

short TO unsigned char
>   Preserve the low-order (rightmost, least significant) byte.

short TO unsigned short
>   Preserve the bit pattern, for example, −1 becomes 65535.

short TO unsigned   Convert to int, convert int to unsigned int.

short TO unsigned long
>   Convert to long, convert long to unsigned long.

int TO char   Preserve the low-order (rightmost, least significant) byte.

int TO short   Identical size.

int TO long   Preserve the signed value.

int TO unsigned char
>   Preserve the low-order (rightmost, least significant) byte.

int TO unsigned short
>   Preserve the bit pattern, for example, −1 becomes 65535.

int TO unsigned   Preserve the bit pattern, for example, −1 becomes 65535.

```
int TO unsigned long
```
        Convert to long, convert long to unsigned long.

```
long TO char
```
        Preserve the low-order (rightmost, least significant) byte.

```
long TO short
```
        Preserve the low-order (rightmost, least significant) two bytes.

```
long TO int
```
        Preserve the low-order (rightmost, least significant) two bytes.

```
long TO unsigned char
```
        Preserve the low-order (rightmost, least significant) byte.

```
long TO unsigned short
```
        Preserve the low-order (rightmost, least significant) two bytes.

```
long TO unsigned
```
        Preserve the low-order (rightmost, least significant) two bytes.

```
long TO unsigned long
```
        Preserve the bit pattern.

```
unsigned char TO char
```
        Preserve the bit pattern.

```
unsigned char TO short
```
        Preserve positive value.

```
unsigned char TO int
```
        Preserve positive value.

```
unsigned char TO long
```
        Preserve positive value.

```
unsigned char TO unsigned short
```
        Preserve positive value.

```
unsigned char TO unsigned
```
        Preserve positive value.

```
unsigned char TO unsigned long
```
        Preserve positive value.

```
unsigned short TO char
```
        Preserve the low-order (rightmost, least significant) byte.

```
unsigned short TO short
```
        Preserve the bit pattern.

```
unsigned short TO int
```
        Preserve the bit pattern, for example, 65535 becomes −1.

```
unsigned short TO long
```
        Convert to unsigned long. Convert unsigned long to long.

```
unsigned short TO unsigned char
```
        Preserve the low-order (rightmost, least significant) byte.

```
unsigned short TO unsigned
```
        Preserve positive value.

```
unsigned short TO unsigned long
```
        Preserve positive value.

```
unsigned TO char
```
        Preserve the low-order (rightmost, least significant) byte.

```
unsigned TO short
```
        Preserve the bit pattern, for example, 65535 becomes −1.

```
unsigned TO int
```
        Preserve the bit pattern, for example, 65535 becomes −1.

```
unsigned TO long
```
        Convert to unsigned long. Convert unsigned long to long.

```
unsigned TO unsigned char
```
        Preserve the low-order (rightmost, least significant) byte.

```
unsigned TO unsigned short
```
        Identical size.

```
unsigned TO unsigned long
```
        Preserve positive value.

```
unsigned long TO char
```
        Preserve the low-order (rightmost, least significant) byte.

```
unsigned long TO short
```
        Preserve low-order (rightmost, least significant) two bytes.

unsigned long TO int
> Preserve low-order (rightmost, least significant) two bytes.

unsigned long TO long
> Preserve the bit pattern.

unsigned long TO unsigned char
> Preserve low-order (rightmost, least significant) byte.

unsigned long TO unsigned short
> Preserve low-order (rightmost, least significant) two bytes.

unsigned long TO unsigned int
> Preserve low-order (rightmost, least significant) two bytes.

■ Discussion of problem

PROBLEM 13.1

Write a program to illustrate all the options given in the INTEGER programs, in the one program.

I will not attempt to give an answer, but would comment that obviously the program will need to incorporate options.

Notes

[1]   The output is given as

        ```
        lowInt >= highInt
        ```

because the >= comparison is the reverse of < . If something is not less than it is either equal to or greater than.

[2]   Or, in the case of some IBM mainframes, an EBCDIC character.

[3]   On some computers with, say, bytes of 7 or 9 bits this can differ. Such systems are rare.

Chapter 14

Real numbers

In C we treat characters and other types of integer as variations on one theme: the bit pattern.

The number of bits in a pattern varies depending upon the type of the item, from the (usual) 8 bits for a character to the (common) 32 bits for a long integer.

Floating point numbers are also bit patterns, in that floating point numbers are stored as sequences of bits. However, floating point bit patterns are not immediately obvious in their meaning. This obscurity should be compared with the way in which the values of characters and integers can be interpreted by a simple examination of the appropriate bit pattern.

● float converted to int

Consider the case of the floating point variable floatVar (assumed to be of 32 bits for the purposes of this demonstration), and the long integer longVar (also of 32 bits):

```
float floatVar = 40000;
long longVar;
```

Both variables occupy 4 bytes (32 bits), and we can find the starting address of both by use of the & (address) prefix operator. Declare two pointers to byte locations (a character pointer), and assign an address to each:

```
char *locFloatVar, *locLongVar;
locFloatVar = &floatVar;
locLongVar = &longVar;
```

There are two ways in which we are able to copy the value of floatVar to longVar.

The first way is by straight assignment:

```
longVar = floatVar;
printf("%ld\n", longVar);
```

The second way is to copy the appropriate number, byte by byte (or character by character), thus:

```
*(locLongVar+0) = *(locFloatVar+0);
*(locLongVar+1) = *(locFloatVar+1);
*(locLongVar+2) = *(locFloatVar+2);
*(locLongVar+3) = *(locFloatVar+3);
printf("%ld\n", longVar);
```

The results of the two methods of copying (assignment, and byte by byte) differ.

The first result is intelligible, and the second is not. The exact form of the results will depend upon the system in use, and in fact a long integer may not occupy the same number of bytes as a float for any specific system.

The actual program is little more than a tying together of the above lines:

```
/* C3P FLOATLONG program */

/* Boris Allan */

/*
 * Copy a float to a long, by two methods.
 */
```

```c
#include <stdio.h>

main()
    {
    float floatVar = 40000; long longVar;
/*
 * Note these are pointers to byte locations.
 */
    char *locFloatVar, *locLongVar;

/*
 * Assign the address (&) of the first byte of
 * floatVar to the pointer locFloatVar. Make
 * similar assignment to locLongVar.
 */
    locFloatVar = &floatVar;
    locLongVar = &longVar;
    printf("\nFLOATLONG\n\n");

/* Method 1 */
    longVar = floatVar;
    printf("%ld\n\n", longVar);

/* Method 2 */
    *(locLongVar+0) = *(locFloatVar+0);
    *(locLongVar+1) = *(locFloatVar+1);
    *(locLongVar+2) = *(locFloatVar+2);
    *(locLongVar+3) = *(locFloatVar+3);
    printf("%ld", longVar);
    }
```

For the system in use (4 byte floats, conforming to the IEEE
floating point format, and 4 byte longs using two's complement) the
outcome is:

FLOATLONG

40000

1193033728

That is, the assignment by

```
    longVar = floatVar;
```

produces a correct result of 40000, but byte by byte copying by

```
    *(locLongVar+0) = *(locFloatVar+0);
```

(and so forth) produces a strange result of 1193033728. The values and results for your system will possibly differ for the second method, but your system should produce the same result for the first method.

:::

PROBLEM 14.1

Write a program to investigate the two forms of copying from float to long.

:::

● Union of float and long

The results of PROBLEM 14.1 can help us understand the C data type known as a union.

A union has a format akin to a struct, but — in a union — the fields are alternative designations. For example, it is possible to declare a union named (say) unionTag:

```
union unionTag
    {
    long longField;
    float floatField;
    };
```

That is, there is a union type with a name tag unionTag which has one field. That field can either be considered as a float (the field floatField), or as a long (the field longField).

Here is a program to illustrate the use of a union, which shows why one should steer clear of unions if at all possible:

```
/* C3P UNIONTAG 1 program */

/* Boris Allan */

/*
 * A union of float and long
 */
union unionTag
    {
    long longField;
    float floatField;
    };

main()
    {
    union unionTag *unionPtr, unionName;
    unionPtr->floatField = 40000;
    unionName.floatField = 40000;

    printf("unionPtr->longField %lX\n",
           unionPtr->longField);
    printf("unionName.longField %lX\n",
           unionName.longField);
    }
```

This program assigns the value 40000 to the floatField of a pointer to a unionTag (that is, unionPtr), and assigns the same value to a unionTag variable (that is, unionName).

The output in both cases is via the longField, and the results are:

unionPtr–>longField 471C4000

unionName.longField 471C4000

If the hexadecimal value 471C4000 is compared to the hexadecimal value output as part of the programs in EXAMPLE 14.1, then the explanation is self-evident.

C does not know whether the value stored in the union field is float or long, the C translator depends upon the programmer knowing. If you make a mistake, there will be no complaint from the translator, in that there will be no syntax error.

The program can be slightly modified to illustrate the typedef facility:

```
/* C3P UNIONTAG 2 program */

/* Boris Allan */

/*
 * Use of typedef
 */
typedef union unionType
    {
    long longField;
    float floatField;
    };
```

```
main()
    {
    unionType *unionPtr, unionName;
    unionPtr->floatField = 40000;
    unionName.floatField = 40000;

    printf("unionPtr->longField %lX\n",
            unionPtr->longField);
    printf("unionName.longField %lX\n",
            unionName.longField);
    }
```

The results of UNIONTAG 1 and UNIONTAG 2 are the same.

● sizeof types

We have assumed that the size of the long integer is identical to that of the float, but this is not necessarily the case. The following program investigates the size (in bytes) of the various types, by use of the sizeof() function.

```
/* C3P SIZEOF 1 program */

/* Boris Allan */

/*
 * Investigate the sizeof types
 */

#include <stdio.h>
#define SIZEPR printf("sizeof ")
#define TYPEPR(TYPE) \
        printf(" is %d\n\n", sizeof(TYPE))
```

```
main()
    {
    SIZEPR; printf("char "); TYPEPR(char);

    SIZEPR; printf("short "); TYPEPR(short);

    SIZEPR; printf("int "); TYPEPR(int);

    SIZEPR; printf("long "); TYPEPR(long);

    SIZEPR; printf("float "); TYPEPR(float);

    SIZEPR; printf("double "); TYPEPR(double);

    SIZEPR; printf("unsigned char ");
    TYPEPR(unsigned char);

    SIZEPR; printf("unsigned short ");
    TYPEPR(unsigned short);

    SIZEPR; printf("unsigned int ");
    TYPEPR(unsigned int);

    SIZEPR; printf("unsigned long ");
    TYPEPR(unsigned long);
    }
```

The output will depend upon the implementation of data types for your system, so first examine the nature of output as given in this program. For example, consider the segment

```
SIZEPR;
printf("unsigned short "); TYPEPR(unsigned short);
```

which is expanded by the preprocessor to give three printf() commands, of which the only unusual feature is the use of the sizeof() facility. That is:

```
printf("sizeof "); printf("unsigned short ");
printf(" is %d\n\n", sizeof(unsigned short));
```

sizeof() returns a value, which is equal to the number of bytes needed to store a variable of the type given. The output will depend upon the implementation of data types. For the system used in this chapter (Microsoft C) the program output is

sizeof char is 1

sizeof short is 2

sizeof int is 2

sizeof long is 4

sizeof float is 4

sizeof double is 8

sizeof unsigned char is 1

sizeof unsigned short is 2

sizeof unsigned int is 2

sizeof unsigned long is 4

Note that it is not possible to have an unsigned float or an unsigned double, and on some systems char will be equivalent to unsigned char in nature, because all char values will be unsigned for that system.

Note, in addition, the identity of the lengths of the signed and unsigned versions of the same type (for example, int and unsigned int). In certain implementations there is no provision, for example, for an unsigned long. Recommendations for the ISO standards include the new type long double.

● Real and integer arithmetic

We have seen'that there are rules which define the form of conversion
between different sizes of bit pattern, and now we will study
conversion between floating point and integer variables. The first
program to assist in this exploration is FLOATINT 1:

```
/* C3P FLOATINT 1 program */

/* Boris Allan */

/*
 * Aspects of real and integer arithmetic.
 * Macro TRIAL(ARG) saves typing.
 */

#include <stdio.h>
#define FIRST 100/3
#define SECOND 100/3.
#define THIRD 100./3

#define PRINT \
    printf("\n%f %f %ld %d\n",\
        doubleNo, floatNo, longNo, intNo)
#define TRIAL(ARG)\
    doubleNo = ARG;\
    floatNo = ARG;\
    longNo = ARG;\
    intNo = ARG;\
    PRINT
```

```
main()
  {
  double doubleNo;
  float floatNo;
  long longNo;
  int intNo;
  printf("\nFLOATINT 1\n");
  TRIAL(FIRST);
  TRIAL(SECOND);
  TRIAL(THIRD);
  }
```

This program makes extensive use of macro definitions (#define) and this brings us to the next problem.

::

PROBLEM 14.2

Expand the program FLOATINT 1 to source code, as would bo produced after the preprocessor pass.

::

What happens is that there are three TRIAL(ARG)s, where the ARG can be either the same as FIRST, SECOND, or THIRD.

Each of the ARGs represents one formula (100/3, 100/3., or 100./3), and the TRIAL() consists of assigning the ARG to each of four variables, plus a PRINT.

PRINT is defined as printing out the four variables.

The reason we start with FIRST is that the formula 100/3 returns an integer result, because both 100 and 3 are assumed by the C translator to be integral. The two constants are assumed to be integral because neither has any explicit fractional part.

The SECOND formula 100/3. returns a real value because 3. is considered to be a real number due to the decimal point (3 is integral, and 3. is real).

The term real, covering both float and double types, is used because the C translator automatically converts all floats into doubles in arithmetic formulae [1]. The result of 100/3. is (therefore) double — see the previous chapter concerning the conversion sequence [2].

In the case of the THIRD formula (100./3) the real constant 100. is of type double, and the type of 3 is integer – but 3 is promoted to double.

The results?

FLOATINT 1

33.000000 33.000000 33 33

33.333333 33.333332 33 33

33.333333 33.333332 33 33

In the FIRST computation all variables have an integral value. That is, all the variables have the value 33, because (int) 100/3 is equal to 33, and not equal to 33.333...

In the case of the SECOND formula, the two types of integer still have the value 33, whereas the two real types have approximations to 33.333... Note that the doubleNo variable has the output value 33.333333 but the floatNo has the value 33.333332. The number of significant digits for doubleNo can be increased, and the result still seems correct, but floatNo is already in error.

For a float variable with a sizeof 4, the number of digits which can be trusted as accurate in any calculation is no more than 7 (and often less). The first 7 digits of floatNo are 33.33333, which is accurate as such.

As will be seen later, the seeming accuracy of the doubleNo is beguiling: the doubleNo is more accurate but not totally accurate (approximately 15 digits accuracy for this implementation).

The THIRD formula gives exactly the same results as the SECOND.

■ Discussion of problems

:::

PROBLEM 14.1

Write a program to investigate the two forms of copying from float to long.

:::

To help to understand the operation of the above program, the program can be extended to provide more information on what has taken place:

```
/* C3P PROBLEM 14.1.1 program */

/* Boris Allan */

/*
 * Copy a float to a long, extended program.
 */

#include <stdio.h>

main()
    {
    float floatVar = 40000;
    long longVar;
    char *locFloatVar, *locLongVar;

    locFloatVar = &floatVar;
    locLongVar = &longVar;
    printf("\nPROBLEM 14.1.1\n\n");
    longVar = floatVar;
```

```
/*
 * Print longVar: first as a long decimal,
 * and then as a long hexadecimal number.
 */
    printf("%ld  %lX\n\n", longVar, longVar);
/*
 * As each byte is transferred, print its value
 * as an hexadecimal number from 00 to FF
 */
    *(locLongVar+0) = *(locFloatVar+0);
       printf("%X\n", *(locFloatVar+0));
    *(locLongVar+1) = *(locFloatVar+1);
       printf("%X\n", *(locFloatVar+1));
    *(locLongVar+2) = *(locFloatVar+2);
       printf("%X\n", *(locFloatVar+2));
    *(locLongVar+3) = *(locFloatVar+3);
       printf("%X\n\n", *(locFloatVar+3));
    printf("%ld  %lX", longVar, longVar);
    }
```

The main difference between the two programs comes from the use of
the print format controls %lX and %X (print as a long hexadecimal
number using upper case, print as a hexadecimal number using upper
case).

The program line:

```
    printf("%ld  %lX\n\n", longVar, longVar);
```

prints out the value of longVar according to the two different
formats. First, longVar is output as a long decimal number (%ld),
and, second, longVar is output as a long hexadecimal number using
upper case letters (%lX). The number is output in a hexadecimal form
because each hex digit is equivalent to a 4 bit binary number [3].

In the portion of program labelled

```
/*
 * As each byte is transferred, print its value
 * as an hexadecimal number from 00 to FF
 */
```

the value transferred is output as a hexadecimal value, so that after transferring the value stored in the second byte of floatVar by

```
*(locLongVar+1) = *(locFloatVar+1);
```

we print out that value by the program line

```
printf("%X\n", *(locFloatVar+1));
```

That is, print according to the %X format the byte (character) value stored in the location (locFloatVar+1). The location locFloatVar is the first byte of the floating point variable floatVar because of the earlier assignment

```
locFloatVar = &floatVar;
```

where &floatVar gives the address of the first location of floatVar. The result of running this program is the output

PROBLEM 14.1.1

40000   0C40

0
40
1C
47

1193033728   471C4000

Note that the transferred decimal number is 1193033728, which bears no relationship to the value 40000. If the hexadecimal values of the separate bytes for the transferred value are examined (00, 40, 1C, and 47, going from the byte in the lower location to the higher byte) it can be seen that these are the bytes in the hex equivalent of 1193033728 (that is, 471C4000).

This equivalence is made clearer if the hexadecimal value is separated into individual byte values (that is, 47 1C 40 00). Note the order in which the bytes are stored in the long integer, that is, the most significant (higher order, leftmost) byte is stored in the location with the highest value address — on other systems the reverse may be true.

:::

PROBLEM 14.2

Expand the program FLOATINT 1 to source code, as would be produced after the preprocessor pass.

:::

Ignoring unnecessary aspects of stdio.h and concentrating on main(), the result after the preprocessor pass is

```
main()
    {
    double doubleNo;
    float floatNo;
    long longNo;
    int intNo;

    printf("\nFLOATINT 1\n");

    doubleNo = 100/3;
    floatNo = 100/3;
    longNo = 100/3;
    intNo = 100/3;
    printf("\n%f %f %ld %d\n",
        doubleNo, floatNo, longNo, intNo);
```

```
doubleNo = 100/3.;
floatNo = 100/3.;
longNo = 100/3.;
intNo = 100/3.;
printf("\n%f %f %ld %d\n",
    doubleNo, floatNo, longNo, intNo);


doubleNo = 100./3;
floatNo = 100./3;
longNo = 100./3;
intNo = 100./3;
printf("\n%f %f %ld %d\n",
    doubleNo, floatNo, longNo, intNo);
}
```

This listing indicates that four variables (of differing types) have the same value assigned and the result of the assignments are output. There are three different values assigned (100/3, 100/3., and 100./3).

Notes

[1]   There has been some debate about this automatic promotion, partly because it is more expensive in terms of resources. New standards for C, therefore, do not have automatic conversion.

[2]   Remember that if the assumed type of the constant value 3. is double, then the integer constant 100 is promoted to double, because 3. is already of type double.

[3]   Note, for example, that the hexadecimal digit uppercase F can also be given as the lowercase f. If the format control is %X then F is output, whereas if the format control is %x then f is output.

Chapter 15

Number conversions

In this chapter we begin to examine how arithmetic is performed in C. The results given in this chapter may not hold for your system, because some of the calculations depend on the order in which operations occur.

This is an important chapter because it helps you to begin to understand how your version of C disentangles sense from expressions.

● Simple accuracy

The problem of accuracy is taken further in the program FLOATINT 2

```
/* C3P FLOATINT 2 program */

/* Boris Allan */

/*
 * Printing reals with more detail (see the
 * definitions for PRECISION, and PRINT).
 */
```

```
#include <stdio.h>
#define FIRST 100/3
#define SECOND 100/3.
#define THIRD 100./3
#define PRECISION 12
#define PRINT \
    printf("\n%.*f %.*f %ld %d\n",\
        PRECISION, dblNo, PRECISION, fltNo,\
        longNo, intNo)
#define TRIAL(ARG)\
    dblNo = ARG;\
    fltNo = ARG;\
    longNo = ARG;\
    intNo = ARG;\
    PRINT

main()
    {
    double dblNo;
    float fltNo;
    long longNo;
    int intNo;

    printf("\nFLOATINT 2\n");

    TRIAL(FIRST);
    TRIAL(SECOND);
    TRIAL(THIRD);
    }
```

As is indicated in the initial comments, the main difference comes in
the new definition of PRECISION, and the changed definition of
PRINT. The main() function (after preprocessing) is similar to the
previous source listing: for example, the equivalent of the command

```
    TRIAL(FIRST);
```

is the expanded set of lines

```
dblNo = 100/3;
fltNo = 100/3;
longNo = 100/3;
intNo = 100/3;
printf("\n%.*f %.*f %ld %d\n",
    12, dblNo, 12, fltNo,
    longNo, intNo);
```

Before we explain the new form of format control (that is, %.*f), here is the output from this program:

FLOATINT 2

33.000000000000 33.000000000000 33 33

33.333333333333 33.333332061768 33 33

33.333333333333 33.333332061768 33 33

● Format control for numerical precision

Consider the PRINT, which is expanded to

```
printf("\n%.*f %.*f %ld %d\n",
    12, dblNo, 12, fltNo,
    longNo, intNo);
```

(Note that there may be small variations in the format controls for printf() on your C system, so check your documentation.)
   There are three different format controls in the above printf() command:

%.*f   This control is repeated twice (for dblNo and fltNo) and outputs a real number (the ´f´) with a specified number of decimal digits after the fractional point. The number of digits is defined by the ´.*´ prefix to f, the number of digits is given as an argument.

Another way of defining 12 digits is by use of the explicit control by `%.12f` but, however, this is less general than using a a macro value in the argument list.

%ld   Output a value assumed to be a long decimal number (signed long integer).

%d   Output a value assumed to be a decimal number (signed integer).

Astute readers will be asking the key question concerning the %.*f and %.12f formats:

::

PROBLEM 15.1

What is wrong with the revised macro definitions

```
#define PREC 12
#define PRINT \
    printf("\n%.PRECf %.PRECf %ld %d\n",\
        dblNo, fltNo, longNo, intNo)
```

to give 12 digits precision?

::

The key line of printed output from FLOATINT 2 (as far as our discussion of accuracy is concerned) is

33.333333333333 33.333332061768 33 33

which shows that the dblNo appears to be totally accurate to 14 significant digits (2 + 12), whereas the accuracy of fltNo is no better than 7 significant digits (2 + 5).

Note that even though the accuracy ends after 7 digits, it is possible to output far more than 7 digits, giving a form of spurious precision. Even though we can give fltNo to 14 digits, the last 7 digits are spurious.

● Storing values

The mixing of types of variable can produce some intriguing results, but first (given your increasing expertise with expanding macro definitions) here is a program which should help clarify certain aspects of the previous problems in this chapter.

::

PROBLEM 15.2

Expand the macro definitions in the following program, and outline the form of output.

```
/* C3P PROBLEM 15.2.1 program */

/* Boris Allan */

/*
 * A mystery
 */

#include <stdio.h>

#define QUOTE "
#define WS 8
#define WD 8
#define PR(NAME) \
      printf("%*s%*d\n", WS, QUOTE NAME", \
          WD, sizeof(NAME))
```

```
main()
  {
  printf("%*s%*s\n\n", WS, "TYPE", WD, "BYTES");

  PR(char);
  PR(short);
  PR(int);
  PR(long);
  PR(float);
  PR(double);
  }
```

:::

In chapter 13 the general rules for deciding upon the type of an expression were given — repeated here:

1. any operands of type char or short are converted to int,

2. any operands of type unsigned char or unsigned short are converted to unsigned int, and

3. any operands of type float are converted to double,

4. IF the type of either operand is double, the other operand is converted to double, and that is the type of the result of the operation, ELSE

5. IF the type of either operand is unsigned long, the other operand is converted to unsigned long, and that is the type of the result of the operation, ELSE

6. IF the type of either operand is long, the other operand is converted to long, and that is the type of the result of the operation, ELSE

7. IF either operand is unsigned int, the other operand is converted to unsigned int, and that is the type of the result of the operation, ELSE

8. both operands are int, and that is the type of the result of the operation.

We gave also an extensive list of conversions between the integral (bit pattern) types and conversions from integral types to reals, which we will not repeat, so all that is left are rules for conversion from real types to integral types:

float TO char	Convert to long, then convert long to char.
float TO short	Convert to long, then convert long to short.
float TO int	Convert to long, then convert long to int.
float TO long	Truncate at decimal point, if result is too large then result is undefined.
float TO unsigned short	Convert to long, then convert long to unsigned short.
float TO unsigned	Convert to long, then convert long to unsigned.
float TO unsigned long	Convert to long, then convert long to unsigned long.
float TO double	Change internal representation.
double TO char	Convert to float, then convert float to char.
double TO short	Convert to float, then convert float to short.
double TO int	Convert to float, then convert float to int.
double TO long	Truncate at decimal point, if result is too large then result is undefined.
double TO unsigned short	Convert to long, then convert long to unsigned short.
double TO unsigned	Convert to long, then convert long to unsigned.
double TO unsigned long	Convert to long, then convert long to unsigned long.
double TO float	Represent as a float: if the double value cannot be represented exactly as a float, then there is loss of precision; if the value is too large to be stored as a float, then the result is undefined.

● Number ranges

In C, as with most language translators, the integer types are stored in two's complement form.

- ☐ The range of values for a 2 byte signed integer (short and int in the sizeof() list) is −32768 to +32767. Complete accuracy is thus available only for 4 digit numbers. In other words, all 4 digit numbers can be stored exactly (that is, up to +/− 9999), but only some 5 digit numbers can be stored in an exact form.

- ☐ A 4 byte signed integer (a long in the list of sizeof()s above) has a range of −2147483648 to +2147483647, and so only 9 digits can be stored exactly (that is, up to +/− 999999999).

In general, the importance of recognizing the digits accuracy of a data type is due to the fact that most output is presented in decimal form. It is tempting to believe your arithmetic is more accurate than is truly the case.

When we turn to the storage of noninteger values, it is more common to store real numbers according to the IEEE conventions for floating point numbers. In simple terms, the proposals for real numbers are:

- ☐ For single precison numbers (4 bytes, 32 bits) 1 bit is set aside as a sign bit, 8 bits represent the exponent (taken to the power of 2), plus 23 bits for the mantissa. An extra bit is assumed (because of the normalized form) to produce an effective 24 bit mantissa. The effective 24 bits for the mantissa provide 7 digits accuracy [1].

- ☐ The format for IEEE double precision numbers (8 bytes, 64 bits) is 1 sign bit, an 11 bit exponent, and 52 bit mantissa plus the implied extra bit due to the normalized form. This gives an accuracy of 15 digits.

It is worth checking the format for real numbers on your system, for several reasons.

For example: most special numeric coprocessor extensions for standard microprocessors use the IEEE format (those provided by Intel, Motorola, Zilog, and National Semiconductor, amongst others).

If your system differs, you will need to provide the appropriate calculations for the accuracy of the arithmetic, though it is increasingly the case that implementors of C systems will conform to the IEEE recommendations.

⬤ Conversion between types

It is as well to keep these sizes in mind when trying to predict the output from the next program which examines conversions between real numbers and integers. If you can answer all these conversions correctly (with reasons) then you are doing well.

It may help to be told that 10000/39 = 256.410256410 ... (recurring).

```
/* C3P CONVERSION 1 program */

/* Boris Allan */

/*
 * Conversion between types, and
 * arithmetical expressions
 */

#include <stdio.h>
#define WD 10
#define WF 17
#define PRINT \
    printf("%*f%*f%*ld%*d\n",\
        WF, dblNo, WF, fltNo,\
        WD, longNo, WD, intNo)
#define iToD intNo = longNo = fltNo = dblNo
#define dToI dblNo = fltNo = longNo = intNo
```

```
main()
   {
   double dblNo;
   float fltNo, flt39 = 39;
   long longNo, long100000000 = 100000000;
   int intNo, int10000 = 10000, int39 = 39;

   printf("CONVERSION 1\n\n");
   printf("%*s%*s%*s%*s\n\n",
          WF, "dblNo",
          WF, "fltNo",
          WD, "longNo",
          WD, "intNo");

/* 1 */
   iToD = int10000/int39; PRINT;
   dToI = int10000/int39; PRINT;
   iToD = (double) int10000/int39; PRINT;
   dToI = (double) int10000/int39; PRINT;

   printf("\n");

/* 2 */
   iToD = long100000000/flt39; PRINT;
   dToI = long100000000/flt39; PRINT;
   }
```

The command

```
   dToI = long100000000/flt39;
```

(for example) is expanded by the preprocessor to

```
   dblNo = fltNo = longNo = intNo
       = long100000000/flt39;
```

That is, the long integer variable equal to 100000000 is divided by the floating point variable equal to 39, and the result is assigned to the integer variable intNo. This value is then assigned (in order) to a long integer variable, a float variable, and a double precision variable. The program output is in two sections.

1. The first four lines should provide no problem, as long as you remember that two integer variables produce an integer result unless an explicit cast is applied. The second two lines have such an explicit cast.

2. When a real variable and an integer variable appear in the same expression, then the calculation is performed as if both quantities were real. If a single precision (float) variable appears in an expression, then that quantity is automatically 'promoted' to double precision. This means that the expression on the right hand side of the equality is treated as double precision.

Here is the printed output.

CONVERSION 1

dblNo	fltNo	longNo	intNo
256.000000	256.000000	256	256
256.000000	256.000000	256	256
256.410256	256.410248	256	256
256.000000	256.000000	256	256
2564102.564103	2564102.500000	2564102	8198
8198.000000	8198.000000	8198	8198

The text is explained in this way:

[1] For all this section the key calculation is 10000/39, and for the first two lines the calculation is performed using integer arithmetic, with the result 256.

For the second two lines, the calculation is performed in double precision mode, and in the case of the third line, this accuracy is transmitted to dblNo. When the double value is assigned to fltNo, because of the restricted digits accuracy of fltNo (7 digits), the last two digits are unreliable. longNo and intNo only store the integer value.

2 For the two lines in this section, the result of the double precision expression 100000000/39 is assigned to dblNo, then, with lack of precision, to fltNo, and then, as an integer, to longNo.

As the value being transmitted is outside the range for an int, only the least significant 2 bytes of the value are stored when the quantity is assigned to intNo (to give 8198). If the assignment of the value of the expression was first to intNo, then intNo is 8198 and that is the value transmitted to all other variables.

This last line shows clearly the need to keep track of the size of values to be transmitted, and the assignment should be that given as iToD. That is, in multiple assignments, always assign first to the most accurate variable and then in successive order of accuracy. Remember:

```
intNo = longNo = fltNo = dblNo = value
```

Having examined the above program, and executed it on your system, you are ready to predict the output from a very similar program, CONVERSION 2.

● Further conversions

```
/* C3P CONVERSION 2 program */

/* Boris Allan */

/*
 * Further conversion between types,
 * and arithmetical expressions
 */
```

```c
#include <stdio.h>
#define WD 10
#define WF 17
#define PRINT \
    printf("%*f%*f%*ld%*d\n",\
        WF, dblNo, WF, fltNo,\
        WD, longNo, WD, intNo)
#define iToD intNo = longNo = fltNo = dblNo
#define iToL intNo = dblNo = fltNo = longNo

main()
    {
    double dblNo;
    float fltNo, flt39 = 39;
    long longNo, long100000000 = 100000000;
    int intNo, int10 = 10, int100 = 100,
        int39 = 39;

        printf("%*s%*s%*s%*s\n\n",
            WF, "dblNo",
            WF, "fltNo",
            WD, "longNo",
            WD, "intNo");
        printf("CONVERSION 2\n\n");

/* 1 */
        iToD = (double) int10
            * long100000000/int30;
        PRINT;
        iToL = int10 * long100000000/int39;
        PRINT;
        iToL = int10 * long100000000/flt39;
        PRINT;

        printf("\n");
```

```
/* 2 */
        iToD = (double) int100
            * long100000000/int39;
        PRINT;
        iToL = (double) int100
            * long100000000/int39;
        PRINT;
        iToL = int100 * long100000000/flt39;
        PRINT;
}
```

It can be seen that there are two sections in this program.

⓵ Note that in this section there is a macro definition for iToL, which is equivalent to

```
intNo = dblNo = fltNo = longNo
```

and you should consider why this line has been reordered. Note the similarities, and the differences between this section and the previous section (a factor of int10).

⓶ This section is trickier than it appears, and I will give no help.

Here are the results of the *CONVERSION 2* program:

CONVERSION 2

dblNo	fltNo	longNo	intNo
25641025.641026	25641026.000000	25641025	16449
25641025.000000	25641024.000000	25641025	16449
25641025.000000	25641024.000000	25641025	16449
256410256.410256	256410256.000000	256410256	−32112
256410256.000000	256410256.000000	256410256	−32112
36155523.000000	36155524.000000	36155523	−20349

And here is the explanation, section by section.

[1] It is because of the restricted accuracy of the intNo that it is now the variable to which we make the last assignment (this is why the macro definition iToL was introduced).

The expression is 1000000000/39 in various forms, and – as longNo – it occupies 8 digits, which is close to the limits of accuracy (9 digits) of a long integer. The number 1000000000 has 10 digits, but luckily this number is still within the range of a long int. The results are unexceptional.

[2] The expression for the last section is 10000000000/39 (in various forms), and the important point to notice is that, though both int100 and long100000000 are within bounds, the result of multiplying the two quantities (10000000000) is out of range for a long int.

This explains the last line, an implementation specific result.

The value 10000000000 is truncated because an int and a long in an expression produce a long result. The truncation occurs before the flt39 variable is encountered.

The Microsoft C compiler does not promote the expression as a whole, and the promotion happens only when the float is reached in a left to right evaluation. Other C translators might use a different mode of evaluation, so note that to assume such implementation specific quirks militates against transportable code.

It is a good idea to investigate mixing data types in this manner, to see what are the forms of output for your particular system.

PROBLEM 15.3

What will be the result of

        iToL = int100 * (long100000000/flt39);

and why?

● Parsing expressions

The next program examines variations on the theme of parsing
expressions:

```
/* C3P PARSING program */

/* Boris Allan */

/*
 * Parsing arithmetical expressions
 */

#include <stdio.h>

#define aInt 21
#define bInt 4
#define aFloat 5.0 /* Explicitly fractional */
#define printLhs(LHS) printf("\n%f, LHS)

main()
   {
   float lhsFloat;

   lhsFloat = aInt/bInt * aFloat;
   printLhs(lhsFloat);

   lhsFloat = (aInt/bInt) * aFloat;
   printLhs(lhsFloat);

   lhsFloat = aInt * aFloat/bInt;
   printLhs(lhsFloat);
```

```
lhsFloat = aInt/(bInt/aFloat)
printLhs(lhsFloat);

lhsFloat = (float) aInt/bInt * aFloat;
printLhs(lhsFloat);

lhsFloat = (double) aInt/bInt * aFloat;
printLhs(lhsFloat);

lhsFloat = aInt/ (float) bInt * aFloat;
printLhs(lhsFloat);
}
```

In theory the result for 21/4 * 5 should be 26.25. The output for the above program is:

```
25.000000
25.000000
26.250000
26.250000
26.250000
26.250000
26.250000
```

and the explanation for the different results is left up to you.

Remember, however, the importance of establishing the order of parsing for the expressions. If the results for your system are at variance, parsing takes a different form for your translator — systems vary, so be wary.

◼ Discussion of problems

:::

PROBLEM 15.1

What is wrong with the revised macro definitions

```
#define PREC 12
#define PRINT \
   printf("\n%.PRECf %.PRECf %ld %d\n",\
      dblNo, fltNo, longNo, intNo)
```

to give 12 digits precision?

:::

The reason why this use of macro definitions will not work is because, after preprocessing, the PRINT macro is expanded to

```
printf("\n%.PRECf %.PRECf %ld %d\n",\
      dblNo, fltNo, longNo, intNo)
```

that is, any text within the double quotemarks " " is not altered by the preprocessor, because all strings are protected from change. Some systems may allow such changes, but such a facility is not sensible.

Additionally, if the continuous sequence of characters PRECf is encountered by the preprocessor (and not enclosed in quotes) then the complete sequence is considered as one unit. That is, the sequence PRECf is not spilt into PREC and f, so that the ultimate result is that the translator informs you that there is an undefined identifier PRECf. The PREC and f have to be separated in some way.

It is worth investigating this feature by writing a program to test the status of macro definitions within strings (that is, characters within quotemarks " ") and one simple example is to take FLOATINT 2, modify and simplify that program:

```
/* C3P PROBLEM 15.1.1 program*/

/* Boris Allan */

/*
 * Simplified FLOATINT 2 (note
 * the definition for PRINT).
 */

#include <stdio.h>
#define PRECf 12f
#define PRINT \
    printf("\n%.PRECf %.PRECf %ld %d\n",\
        dblNo, fltNo, longNo, intNo)

main()
    {
    double dblNo = 100/3;
    float fltNo = 100/3;
    long longNo = 100/3;
    int intNo = 100/3;

    printf("\nPROBLEM 15.1.1\n");
    PRINT;
    }
```

where the preprocessed output is

```
main()
  {
  double dblNo = 100/3;
  float fltNo = 100/3;
  long longNo = 100/3;
  int intNo = 100/3;

  printf("\nPROBLEM 15.1.1\n");
  printf("\n%.PRECf %.PRECf %ld %d\n",
      dblNo, fltNo, longNo, intNo);
  }
```

and the display after executing the program is

PROBLEM 15.1.1

PRECf PRECf 0 −32768

That is, the first two format controls, `%.PRECf`, are merely interpreted as injunctions to print PRECf, and the second pair of controls (for decimal integers) are then applied to the first two arguments in the list. As the first two arguments are real numbers, the conversion is byte by byte, producing the strange results as given (see also the discussion of byte transfer in PROBLEM 14.1).

●●●

PROBLEM 15.2

Expand the macro definitions in the following program, and outline the form of output.

```
/* C3P PROBLEM 15.2.1 program */

/* Boris Allan */

/*
 * A mystery
 */
```

```
#include <stdio.h>

#define QUOTE "
#define WS 8
#define WD 8
#define PR(NAME) \
        printf("%*s%*d\n", WS, QUOTE NAME", \
           WD, sizeof(NAME))

main()
    {
    printf("%*s%*s\n\n", WS, "TYPE", WD, "BYTES");

    PR(char);
    PR(short);
    PR(int);
    PR(long);
    PR(float);
    PR(double);
    }
```

The above program will not produce sensible results on all systems because of the crucial sequence:

    QUOTE NAME",

which is part of the argument list for the printf() function.

The macro definition QUOTE is equivalent to ", and — as the next quotemark is after NAME — the substitution is made for both QUOTE and NAME" (where the " at the end of NAME serves as a delimiter).

The preprocessor does not recognize the " as the start of a string, as it is adjacent to NAME, and thus the next substitution

    sizeof(NAME)

is carried out as normal.

The relevant preprocessed output is

```
main()
  {
  printf("%*s%*s\n\n", 8, "TYPE", 8, "BYTES");

  printf("%*s%*d\n",
        8, " char", 8, sizeof(char));
  printf("%*s%*d\n",
        8, " short", 8, sizeof(short));
  printf("%*s%*d\n",
        8, " int", 8, sizeof(int));
  printf("%*s%*d\n",
        8, " long", 8, sizeof(long));
  printf("%*s%*d\n",
        8, " float", 8, sizeof(float));
  printf("%*s%*d\n",
        8, " double", 8, sizeof(double));
  }
```

The output matches that from the earlier sizeof() program, though without the unsigned types. As was noted above:

☐ The sizes of equivalent signed and unsigned types are identical.

☐ Not all systems implement signed and unsigned types for every integral type.

A useful program would be one which input the name of a type (as a string) and then gave the size. See if you can write such a program, for I will not give a solution.

●●●

PROBLEM 15.3

What will be the result of

> iToL = int100 * (long100000000/flt39);

and why?

●●●

The results given here can depend on your version of C, and the way in which conversions are performed. If there are differences when you try the example for yourself, then try to ascertain the reasons for the differences.

The equivalent line in the CONVERSION 2 program is

> iToL = int100 * long100000000/flt39;

and the sequence of evaluation (parsing in reverse Polish) for the original line is

> int100 long100000000 * flt39 /

That is, first the two values are considered, then the values are multiplied, and then the result of the multiplication is divided by flt39.

The parsing of the problem line is altered by the use of the parentheses:

> int100 long100000000 flt39 / *

That is, the expression in parentheses is evaluated first (the division) and the result of the division is multiplied by int100. In this case the first arithmetical operation is the division, which involves a long and a float, so the whole expression is promoted to double. The output is

> *256410256.000000 256410256.000000 256410256   −32112*

which is the same as that produced with an explicit cast to double.

Note

[1]   A convenient rule of thumb is to calculate
        int(numberOfBits * 0.3). Thus

        int(16 * 0.3) = 4

        int(32 * 0.3) = 9, and

        int(24 * 0.3) = 7.

Part Five

Applications

The chapters in this section examine types of applications —
at varying levels of complexity — using C.

Subjects such as program arguments, use of structures, or
manipulation of files, begin to make most sense when seen
in use.

Chapter 16

System calls in C

With its origins as an applications language, C has always taken into account the operating systems and the workings of that operating system — the UNIX operating system is written in C.

Some of the programs in this chapter were originally written in Microsoft C running under MSDOS 3.2, and other programs were written for the standard UNIX C compiler cc, running on a Sun workstation.

The slight differences in output are unimportant.

● Arguments to main( )

When one activates the UNIX C compiler (cc) to (say) compile a program carol.c, the command line is:

cc carol.c

which sends the compiled (executable) output to a default file a.out.

To give the executable file the name carol, the a.out file has to be renamed — with the command line

mv a.out carol

Both cc and mv are *programs* and the names of the files (carol.c, a.out, and carol) are program *arguments*.

Any C program can take arguments on the command line, and the arguments are known (conventionally) as argc and argv. The arguments appear as arguments to the main() function. That is, the declaration is:

```
main(argc,argv)
/* Number of arguments */
int argc;
/* An array of pointers to strings */
char *argv[];
    {
    .
    .
    .
    }
```

The first argument is argc, the count of the number of arguments, and the second argument is argv, an array of argc pointers to strings (where the strings contain the full names of the arguments).

argv[2], say, contains a pointer to the start of the second command line argument. As an array is accessed by pointers, to access the third element of argv we have to point to the location (argv + 2), where the element size is two bytes under MSDOS and four bytes on the Sun 2 (say).

The argv argument to main() (not to be confused with a command line argument) is thus a pointer to pointers to strings, and an alternative declaration is:

```
main(argc,argv)
int argc;
char **argv;
    {
    .
    .
    .
    }
```

● Storing command line arguments

Here is a program to examine the ways in which the arguments are stored in the case of one system (Microsoft C, under MSDOS 3.2).

```
/* C3P ARGTEST PROGRAM */


/* Boris Allan */


/*
 * The storage of program arguments
 */


#include <stdio.h>

main(argc,argv)
int argc;
char *argv[]; /* size given elsewhere */
   {
   do
      {
      argc--;
      printf("%d %s %u %u\n",
            argc, /* argument number */
            argv[argc], /* the argument */
            &argv[argc], /* pointer address */
            argv[argc] /* start address */);
      }
   while (argc != 0) ; /* while arguments left */
   }
```

The result of entering the program name argtest or — because MSDOS is case insensitive — ARGTEST, followed by several arguments is illustrated by:

*C:>*__argtest C3P by Boris Allan__

4 Allan 3608 3656

3 Boris 3606 3650

2 by 3604 3647

1 C3P 3602 3643

0 C:\BORIS\WORKING\ARGTEST.EXE 3600 3612

☐ The argument number for the program name is 0 (this is always true for program names). That is, the first argument is the program name.

☐ The first argument name — argv[0] the name of the program — is C:\BORIS\WORKING\ARGTEST.EXE, output as a string because of the format control %s. The program name argtest is converted to uppercase, the file extension .EXE is appended, and the full path name C:\BORIS\WORKING\ is prepended.

☐ At location 3600 is stored a pointer to the start of the first argument (& argv[argc]).

☐ The string starts at location 3612, that is, argv[0] is output as an integer because of the format control %d.

The length of the string C:\BORIS\WORKING\ARGTEST.EXE is 31 characters including \0. The address of the second argument (argv[1], or C3P) is stored in location 3602 and the content of that location (the value of the pointer) is 3647.

If the first argument starts at location 3612, and the second argument starts at location 3643, the difference between the first locations of the two arguments is 31 bytes. 31 bytes is also the size of the string which contains the first argument.

● Naming the main( ) arguments

The naming of argc and argv in the main() function is purely conventional — as is the naming of arguments for any function — and this is illustrated by an equivalent program which uses two different names for the arguments:

The ARGEST and ARGTEST2 programs give identical results.

```
/* C3P ARGTEST2 PROGRAM */

/* Boris Allan */

/*
 * Alternative argument names for main()
 */

#include <stdio.h>

main(argCount,argVector)
int argCount;
char *argVector[];
   {
   do
      {
      argCount--;
      printf("%d %s %u %u\n",
            argCount, argVector[argCount],
            &argVector[argCount],
            argVector[argCount]);
      }
   while (argCount != 0) ;
   }
```

Finally, before moving to an other aspect of the argv argument, study:

   C:>argtest "C3P by Boris Allan"

   1 C3P by Boris Allan 3606 3642
   0 C:\BORIS\WORKING\ARGTEST.EXE 3604 3610

noting that "C3P by Boris Allan" is treated as one control line argument by the system.

● A two–dimensional array

We have seen that *argv[] can also be declared as **argv: it is possible to consider argv as an irregular (nonrectangular) two-dimensional array.

The next program illustrates this aspect of pointers and arrays:

```
/* C3P 2D-ARRAY PROGRAM */

/* Boris Allan */

/*
 * Treat argVec as a two-dimensional array
 */

#include <stdio.h>

main(argCt,argVec)
int argCt;
char *argVec[];
    {
    int charCt, vecCt = 1;
    while (argCt != vecCt)
        {
        for (charCt = 0;
                putchar(argVec[vecCt][charCt])
                    != '\0';
                charCt++)
            ;
        vecCt++;
        }
    }
```

An example of input and output from 2D-ARRAY is given below. I will leave the explanation of the sequence to you:

*C:>**2darray first second third***
first second third

⬤ A recursive main( ) function

As `main()` is a function like any other, the `main()` function can call
itself. The result of executing the program will depend upon the
system:

```
/* C3P MAINTEST PROGRAM */

/* Boris Allan */

/* A recursive main() function */

#include <stdio.h>

main()
   {
   printf("C3P ");
   main(); /* !!!!! */
   }
```

Under MSDOS we are told there is a stack overflow (after a large
number of calls, flagged by *C3P* being output), and for the Sun there
is the message *core dumped.*

   There is no utility to this program other than enabling you to
investigate your system: systems vary, so be wary.

⬤ System calls

So far we have seen how it is possible to communicate information
from the system to a C program: the next stage is to communicate
information from a C program to the system.

Sending information to the system will be illustrated by the disruptive program `carol`. There are two main versions of this program, where the differences come from the treatment of output to `stdout`.

The `carol` programs are nonrecursive in their definition, but they can be used in a recursive manner: as can all C programs, `carol` is intended as a warning of what can happen when you write programs with too many embedded system calls.

```
/* C3P CAROL 1 PROGRAM */


/* Boris Allan */


/* A system call program */

#include <stdio.h>
/*
 * For Microsoft C
#include <process.h>
 * this version for the Sun 2
 */
main(argCt, argVec)
int argCt;
char *argVec[];
    {
    printf("%s ->", argVec[--argCt]);
    printf("%d\n", system(argVec[argCt]));
    }
```

The principal feature of this program is the line

```
    printf("%d\n", system(argVec[argCt]));
```

which prints the decimal value which is returned by the function `system()` — the value will termed the `errorLevel`. The function `system()` takes a string, and executes that string as a system call. The `errorLevel` returns a value which depends upon the status of the command line argument call.

The returned value (the errorLevel) is 0 if the system call was executed successfully, and a nonzero value if there was an error. If the system is MSDOS (running Microsoft C) then an include file known as process.h is needed.

The examples which follow are for UNIX BSD 4.2 on a Sun 2 Workstation, using the standard C compiler. The program executes the last command line argument as a sytem call, printing out the status of the executed system program after execution. For example:

```
% carol "ls ca*"
carol.c    carol
ls ca*   ->0
```

which executes the UNIX command to list all files starting with **ca**, that is, **ls ca***.

carol can modify herself: for example,

```
1% carol "mv carol carol2"
mv carol carol2  ->0
2% carol "ls ca*"
carol: Command not found
3% carol2 "ls ca*"
carol.c   carol2
ls ca* 0
4%
```

1%   The UNIX command line **mv carol carol2**, renames the program file carol to carol2, that is, carol changes her name to carol2.

2%   The carol program is used to execute the command line ls ca*, but as the program has been renamed we find *carol: Command not found*, and the command line is not executed.

3%   The renamed program carol2 is used to list all files beginning with ca, and we discover the new program name carol2, where before there was carol.

Note that the output occurs after the action of the command line. That is, the instruction to

```
printf("%s ->", argVec[--argCt]);
```

is not executed until after the command line

```
printf("%d\n", system(argVec[argCt]));
```

● Flushing buffers

If a slight modification is made to CAROL 1, that is,

```
/* C3P CAROL 2 PROGRAM */

/* Boris Allan */

/* A second system call program */

#include <stdio.h>

main(argCt, argVec)
int argCt;
char *argVec[];
    {
    printf("%s ->", argVec[--argCt]);
    fflush(stdout); /* flush buffer */
    printf("%d\n", system(argVec[argCt]));
    }
```

the program is far easier to track.
    Consider the command line

```
% carol "ls ca*"
ls ca*  ->carol.c   carol
0
```

and now the echo of the command line argument takes place before
the argument is executed. The 0 in the final line indicates that the
execution of the system command has been successful.
    However, not all systems calls are successful. For example:

```
% carol lm
lm ->sh: lm: not found
256
%
```

which means that the system call lm does not exist. The exit value of 256 indicates unsuccessful completion.

● Recursive carol

A slightly more complex example is:

```
% carol "carol jobs"
carol jobs ->jobs ->sh: jobs: not found
256
0
```

This command line involves a recursive call of carol: the left carol executes the command line argument carol jobs, and that carol (in turn) executes the command line argument jobs.

There is no system call jobs, so the errorLevel is 256, but the call to carol jobs is successful (carol works) and so the errorLevel is 0.

An example of a nested successful command line is

```
% carol "carol whoami"
carol whoami ->whoami ->ballan
0
0
```

and an example of an interesting nested command line is

```
% carol
```

— a successful way of tying a system in knots.

The command line involves a recursive call to carol without any extra arguments, and multiple calls are made to carol from within carol. Finally (it depends on the system), an end is reached with an errorLevel of (frequently) −1.

Chapter 17

File handling — Wordstar

The ease with which files can be handled in C makes many tricky problems simple.

The application area to be studied in this chapter is that of converting files from Wordstar format to ASCII format, and — more interesting from a programming point of view — converting ASCII files to Wordstar format.

The programs herein have been successfully implemented on microcomputers, and as I have yet to see Wordstar on a UNIX system the main application is in the microcomputer area. Users of other systems will find the topic useful in helping to come to terms with the organization of files, as assumed by C.

● File streams and file handles

When we have been talking about the standard data streams in C, we have noted that the three streams stdin, stdout, and stderr, have a number associated with each stream.

Each stream is a pointer to a FILE data structure. That is,

```
FILE *stream;
```

which does not mean that the structure of the physical file on the disk is defined by FILE. The ways in which we describe the current status of the physical file are defined by the FILE data structure.

It is possible to have up to an implementation defined maximum number of files open at any one time: the different streams are elements of an array of type FILE. The element number of a stream in the array is known as the device number or — more commonly — the file handle.

Here are the three distinctions to remember:

[1] The physical file;

[2] The stream (a pointer to a data structure); and

[3] The element number of the array of data structures (the file handle).

C systems have library functions and macros which enable the programmer to move between handle and stream. Different file functions require different file descriptions: sometimes the stream, sometimes the handle.

For example, in Microsoft C a macro is defined in `stdio.h` which converts from a stream to a handle: that is

```
int fileno(FILE *);
```

Normally, functions which use the stream designation are higher level routines (they use automatic buffering, and so forth), whereas functions using file handles are low level routines.

● Wordstar files

Wordstar is a very common word processor on microcomputers (probably the most widely available of all word processors). The information about the text is stored in a special format, and the text is not saved as conventional ASCII file.

Wordstar deals in paragraphs, where the end of a paragraph is signalled by a "hard" carriage return (that is, ASCII 13). The end of each physical line of text is signalled by a "soft" carriage return (that is, ASCII 141). The end of line soft carriage return is preceded by a space (that is, ASCII 32).

The end of each word is signalled by the bit for the final character being set high. The conversion program assumes that the Wordstar file is reasonably uncomplicated, and that no extra formatting codes have been introduced.

Note that individual characters are sent as octal values by use of the escape symbol \.

```
/* C3P MAKE ASCII PROGRAM */

/* Boris Allan */

/* Converting from Wordstar file,
 * removing soft characters
 */

#include <stdio.h>

/*
 * End of file is EOF or control Z
 * Note that control Z is denary 26,
 * and octal 32
 */
#define endOfFile(IN) \
          (( IN == EOF) || (IN == '\32'))
FILE *setFilePtr(argPos, argVec,
     accessType)
int argPos;
char *argVec, *accessType;
   {
   FILE *filePtr;

   if ((filePtr = fopen(argVec[argPos],
       accessType)) == NULL)
     {
     fprintf(stderr, "File error on %d",
         argPos);
     exit (argPos);
     }
   else
     return (filePtr);
   }
```

```
main(argCt, argVec)
int argCt;
char *argVec[];
    {
    FILE *fPtrIn, *fPtrOut,
        *setPtr(int, char **, char *);
    int inChar;

    fPtrIn = setFilePtr(1, argVec, "rb");
    fPtrOut = setFilePtr(2, argVec, "wb");

    while (! endOfFile(inChar = fgetc(fPtrIn))
        fputc(inChar & 127, fPtrOut);

    fcloseall();
    exit 0;
    }
```

In essence, the function setFilePtr() returns a pointer to a stream, and takes three arguments — the first two arguments choose the file name, and the third argument establishes the type of access to the named file.

A file can be opened as ready reading, writing, appending, or reading and writing: there will be slight variations on the form of the fopen() function depending on the system.

A file can be opened in either translated or binary mode. If a file is opened in translated mode, the carriage return/linefeed combination is treated as one unit. If in binary mode, the carriage return is treated as one item, and the linefeed is another item.

To convert from a file which has soft returns to a file with hard returns the files have to be opened in binary mode. In the fopen() routine, rb means read in binary, and wb means write in binary. The value returned from fopen() is a pointer to a file (the stream): if the file cannot be opened, a NULL pointer is returned.

What happens is that

☐ a stream of bytes is read (by use of fgetc(fPtrIn)),

☐ the value is checked for end of file (defined in a macro endOfFile()), and

☐ the value is output to another stream with the most significant bit set to 0 (by use of fputc(inChar & 127, fPtrOut)).

To convert from a Wordstar file text.doc to a file text.txt, the command line is

fromws text.doc   text.txt

I leave you to investigate the finer points of error checking.

● Making Wordstar files

Converting from ordinary ASCII files to Wordstar format files is slightly more complex than the reverse operation, but assisted by the fact that the last characters in words need not have their high bit set.

The input (ASCII) file has to signal the end of paragraphs by a double hard return, and so the program logic has to be able to distinguish between single returns (which are sent as soft returns), and double returns (which are sent as hard returns). Note that the input file is opened in translated mode (rt or r).

The program is left as an example for study:

```
/* C3P MAKE WORDSTAR PROGRAM */

/* Boris Allan */

/* Converting to Wordstar file,
 * adding soft characters.
 */

#include <stdio.h>
```

```
#define endOfFile(IN) \
          (( IN == EOF) || (IN == ´\32´))
#define eqNL(IN) IN == ´\n´
#define hardNL(IN) fprintf(IN, "\15\12")
#define softNL(IN) fprintf(IN, "\40\215\12")
#define CLOSE(STREAM) \
          fputc(´\32´, STREAM); fcloseall()


FILE *setFilePtr(argPos, argVec,
     accessType)
int argPos;
char *argVec, *accessType;
   {
   FILE *filePtr;

   if ((filePtr = fopen(argVec[argPos],
        accessType)) == NULL)
     {
     fprintf(stderr, "File error on %d",
          argPos);
     exit (argPos);
     }
   else
     return (filePtr);
   }
```

```
main(argCt, argVec)
int argCt;
char *argVec[];
  {
  FILE *fPtrIn, *fPtrOut,
        *setPtr(int, char **, char *);
  int aChar = '\n', bChar, cChar;

  fPtrIn = setFilePtr(1, argVec, "r");
  fPtrOut = setFilePtr(2, argVec, "wb");

  for (bChar = fgetc(fPtrIn);
       ! endOfFile(cChar = fgetc(fPtrIn));
       aChar = bChar, bChar = cChar)
    {
    if (eqNL(bChar))
      {
      if (eqNL(aChar))
        hardNL(fPtrOut);
      else
        {
        if (eqNL(cChar))
          hardNL(fPtrOut);
        else
          softNL(fPtrOut);
        }
      }
    else
      fputc(bChar, fPtrOut);
    }
  fputc(bChar, fPtrOut);
  CLOSE(fPtrOut);
  }
```

Remember that octal \15 (say) is equivalent to denary 13.

Chapter 18

Constructing linked lists

In C, the memory is not allocated by some magical device: the programmer has to keep track of allocation, and perform the allocating.

The LINKLIST program is a simple example of memory allocation, illustrated by means of a structure linkList

```
struct linkList
    {
    char *name;
    struct linkList *next;
    } ;
```

That is, the structure linkList consists of two fields: name, a pointer to a character; and next, a pointer to a struct linkList. Each field is a pointer: for the field to point to something sensible, therefore, memory has to be allocated.

● malloc( ) and calloc( )

Memory can be allocated in an explicit manner by two functions, malloc() and calloc().

The declaration of calloc() is

```
char *calloc(n, size)
unsigned n; /* number of elements */
unsigned size; /* number of bytes per element */
```

Allocate n * size bytes of memory, and return a character pointer
to the first location of the memory allocated. Often the value of each
byte is set to zero. To return a pointer of a different type use a cast.

malloc() allocates a block of memory, but memory is not
initialized, and the numbers of elements is taken to be one:

```
char *malloc(size)
unsigned size; /* number of bytes */
```

To allocate memory for an instance of the structure linkList we
enter

```
struct linkList exampleElement;
exampleElement = (struct linkList *) /* cast */
       malloc(sizeof(struct linkList)); /* size */
```

exampleElement now points to the start of a portion of memory,
where the memory allocated is the sizeof(struct linkList). For
both functions, if memory cannot be released then a NULL pointer is
returned.

Note that even strings need memory allocated, unless the allocation
is part of a declaration or initialization.

● Linked lists

The LINKLIST program allocates memory for the next field of
structure, and for the name field. The malloc() function is declared
in the header file malloc.h, and the string functions are declared in
a file strings.h.

On some systems there may be no need for either or both of these
header files — the information may be contained in stdio.h — and
so when compiling this program keep these points in mind.

```
/* C3P LINKLIST PROGRAM */

/* Boris Allan */

/*
 * Allocating memory for structures
 * and strings
 */

#include <stdio.h>
#include <malloc.h>
#include <strings.h>

#define LLALLOC (struct linkList *) \
          malloc(sizeof(struct linkList))

struct linkList
   {
   char *name;
   struct linkList *next;
   };

typedef struct linkList *LLIST;

LLIST succ(now) /* find the next element */
LLIST now;
   {
   printf("%s\n", now->name);
   return(now->next);
   }
```

```
char *strdup(inStr) /* duplicate string return
                            starting location */
char *inStr;
  {
  char *aStr;
  printf("sizeof %s is %u\n",
       inStr, strlen(inStr));
  aStr = calloc(strlen(inStr) + 1, 1);
  strcpy(aStr, inStr);
  return(aStr);
  }

main()
  {
  char *strdup();
  LLIST first, second, third, last, temp;

  printf("sizeof linkList is %u\n",
       sizeof(struct linkList));

  temp = LLALLOC; first = LLALLOC;
  temp->next = first;
  first->name = strdup("one");

  second = LLALLOC; first->next = second;
  second->name = strdup("two");

  third = LLALLOC; second->next = third;
  third->name = strdup("three");
```

```
last = LLALLOC; third->next = last;
last->name = strdup("four");
last->next = NULL;

do
    temp->next = succ(temp->next);
while (temp->next != NULL);
}
```

Note that pointers on the system used are of four bytes. The output is:

sizeof linkList is 8
sizeof one is 3
sizeof two is 3
sizeof three is 5
sizeof four is 4
one
two
three
four

In the above program, the line

```
second = LLALLOC; first->next = second;
```

can be replaced by

```
first->next = (second = LLALLOC);
```

and this might give you an idea for a function ...

Chapter 19

Statistics and numerical accuracy

In this chapter the intention is

- ☐ to show how numerical accuracy can be improved by careful choice of numerical algorithm, and
- ☐ to indicate how a program can be written to take into account different possible modes of input.

The analysis will concentrate on the calculation of the means of, the standard deviations of, and the correlation between, two pairs of values. The first pair of values is X = {0 5 8}, and Y = {5 8 0}, and the second pair is X = {1000000 1000005 1000008}, and Y – {1000005 1000008 1000000}.

The means for the first pair of variables are 4.333333333 (for each variable), and the standard deviations are 3.299831646 (using a calculator). The means for the second set are 1000004.333 and the standard deviations are both 0.0 — the result for the standard deviation is incorrect. The calculator is wrong.

◉ Accumulating sums

In bivariate statistics three types of sum are accumulated:

- ① The sum of individual values, to produce the mean;
- ② The sum of squared values, to produce the variance after manipulation; and
- ③ The sum of crossproducts, to produce the covariance after manipulation.

The values X = {1000000 1000005 1000008}, and Y = {1000005 1000008 1000000} give strange results because the variations between the values are very small compared to the absolute size of the values.

A common way to calculate the mean is to sum all the values, and divide by the number of different instances. There are problems with this method when implemented on a computer, because a small number (the latest value) is being added to a large number (the current sum).

A method which is not so susceptible to rounding errors is to take the mean so far, and calculate the current mean when the latest value is taken into account. That is:

```
newMeanX = (numVals * oldMeanX + inX)
    /(numVals + 1);
```

Or, the new mean for X is equal to the old mean for X multiplied by the number of values used to calculate the old mean, plus the input value for X, all divided by the number of values including the current input value.

The current sum of squares around the mean (for X) can be calculated by the formula

```
sumXX += (inX - newMeanX) * (inX - oldMeanX);
```

with an equivalent formula for the crossproduct for X and Y:

```
sumXY += (inX - newMeanX) * (inY - oldMeanY);
```

Conventionally, the calculation of the sum of squares around the mean is left until all the values have been read. As each value is input the sum of squares is accumulated:

```
sumOfSquaresX += inX * inX;
```

and after the values have been read:

```
sumXX = sumOfSquaresX/numVals;
```

This technique is much less accurate: write a program to check this out.

● Varying forms of input and output

Let the statistics program be stored as the executable file stats. On UNIX or MSDOS, there are two ways of providing input to the program:

[1] Input can come from the standard input stream stdin, directly at the keyboard or by redirection; or

[2] Input can come from a named file given as an argument.

That is:

stats	Expect the input from the keyboard (stdin).
stats < data	Expect the data from the file data by redirection (stdin).
program | stats	Expect the data as a result of executing the command program (piping).
stats data	Expect the data from the file data, given as the first argument.

Note that if the standard input stream is used, then there is no extra argument (< data does not count as an argument).

The function FILE *setFilePtr(num, vec) sets the input stream either to stdin or to the file named as the argument. The content of this function is similar to those given earlier (in chapter 17).

Output from the program is always to the standard output channel (stdout) which can be piped or redirected if using the UNIX or MSDOS operating systems. For example,

stats	Print results on screen (stdout)
stats > listing	Send the results to the file listing.
stats | lpr	Send the results to the printer (piping).

This means that input can be piped to the program, and output can also be piped.

⬤ The stats program

The aim of this program is not only to provide an accurate algorithm, but also to allow a check on the effects of float versus double accumulators (declared as REAL).

```c
/* C3P STATS PROGRAM */

/* Boris Allan */

/*
 * Bivariate statistics using
 * running mean algorithms
 */

#include <stdio.h>
#include <math.h>

/*
 * REAL can also be double to check
 * the affects of accumulators
 * of differing precision
 */
#define REAL float
#define PRECISION 12
#define PR(LABEL, VARIABLE)\
        printf("%s %.*G\n",\
        LABEL, PRECISION, \
        VARIABLE)
```

```c
/*
 * Establish source of input,
 * that is, the name of the stream
 */
FILE *setFilePtr(num, vec)
int num;
char *vec[];
    {
    FILE *filePtr;

    if (num == 1)
        return (stdin);
    else
        {
        if ((filePtr = fopen(vec[1],"r")) == NULL)
            {
            fprintf(stderr, "Unknown file error");
            exit (1);
        }
        else
            return(filePtr);
        }
    }

main(argC, argV)
int argC;
char *argV[];
    {
/*
 * Accumulators - change the #define REAL
 * to alter accuracy
 */
    REAL oldMeanX, oldMeanY, newMeanX,
          newMeanY, sumXY, sumXX, sumYY,
          varX, varY, sdX, sdY, covXY,
          corrXY;
```

```
float inX, inY;
int numVals;
FILE *filePtr;

filePtr = setFilePtr(argC, argV);

for (oldMeanX = oldMeanY = sumXY
        = sumXX = sumYY = numVals
        = 0 ;
    EOF != fscanf(filePtr, "%f%f",
        &inX, &inY) ;
    numVals++ )
  {
  newMeanX = (numVals * oldMeanX + inX)
        /(numVals + 1);
  newMeanY = (numVals * oldMeanY + inY)
        /(numVals + 1);
  sumXY += (inX - newMeanX)
        * (inY - oldMeanY);
  sumXX += (inX - newMeanX)
        * (inX - oldMeanX);
  sumYY += (inY - newMeanY)
        * (inY - oldMeanY);
  oldMeanX = newMeanX;
  oldMeanY = newMeanY;
  }

if (numVals == 0)
  {
  fprintf(stderr, "File empty");
  exit (2);
  }
```

```
varX = sumXX/numVals;
sdX = sqrt((double) varX);
varY = sumYY/numVals;
sdY = sqrt((double) varY);
covXY = sumXY/numVals;
corrXY = sumXY
        / sqrt((double) sumXX * sumYY);


PR("mean X ", newMeanX);
PR("mean Y ", newMeanY);
PR("S Dev X", sdX);
PR("S Dev Y", sdY);
PR("Covar  ", covXY);
PR("Correl ", corrXY);
}
```

● Program results (Sun 2 Workstation)

The first set of results are those for REAL being float — with the same results being produced by the ordinary method:

mean X	4.33333349228
mean Y	4.33333349228
S Dev X	3.2998316288
S Dev Y	3.2998316288
Covar	− 5.44444417953
Correl	−0.499999970198

The data is contained in a file in this form:

0 5 5 8 8 0

The next results are those for the same data, but with REAL being double:

mean X	*4.33333333333*
mean Y	*4.33333333333*
S Dev X	*3.29983164554*
S Dev Y	*3.29983164554*
Covar	*−5.44444444444*
Correl	*−0.5*

Note the change in accuracy produced by the improved precision accumulators.

For the data set

```
1000000 1000005
1000005 1000008
1000008 1000000
```

the results using float are

mean X	*1000004.3125*
mean Y	*1000004.3125*
S Dev X	*3.30561375618*
S Dev Y	*3.29298496246*
Covar	*−5.48958349228*
Correl	*−0.504309892654*

and it can be seen that the accuracy is less than before. Even with double, the results show a decline (relative to the earlier set with double). That is,

mean X	*1000004.33333*
mean Y	*1000004.33333*
S Dev X	*3.29983164553*
S Dev Y	*3.29983164555*
Covar	*−5.44444444436*
Correl	*−0.499999999992*

The decline is, however, minimal.

If the standard method is used with double accumulators, the output is:

mean X	1000004.33333
mean Y	1000004.33333
S Dev X	3.29981725938
S Dev Y	3.29981725938
Covar	−5.44458007813
Correl	−0.500016815955

which shows a further decline in accuracy

If the second set of values are used with a standard method and float accumulators, then the correlation is given as 1.0, and the standard deviations are large values (208.525...) — a situation which might lead to gross errors in interpretation, for the unawares.

Operator precedence

Primary operators

    [ ]
    (   )
    . (field selector, structure)
    -> (field selector, pointer to structure)

All have highest (and equal) priority, grouping left to right.

Unary operator

    * (content of)
    & (address of)
    - (unary minus)
    ! (logical NOT)
    ~ (bitwise NOT)
    ++ (increment)
    -- (decrement)
    sizeof( )
    (typeName) (cast)

Have lower priority than the primary operators, but higher than
than any binary operators, they group right to left.

Binary operator

    multiplicationOp   highest priority
    additionOp
    bitShiftOp
    comparisonOp

```
equalityOp
```
& (bitwise AND)
^ (bitwise ^ XOR)
| (bitwise OR)
&& (logical AND)
|| (logical OR)
? : (assignment operator)   lowest priority

```
Group left to right.
```

Multiplication operator

```
*
/
% (remainder)
```

Addition operator

```
+
−
```

Bit shift operator

>> (shift LHS right RHS bits)
<< (shift LHS left RHS bits)

Comparison operator

```
<
>
<=
>=
```

Equality operator

```
==
!=
```

Assignment operator

```
=
+=
-=
*=
/=
%=
>>=
<<=
&=
^=
|=
```

All have equal (and lowest) priority.

Index